Colin Sutherland PhD was a Principal Lecturer at the University of Central Lancashire. On leaving the university he worked for ten years as a psychotherapist using techniques of counselling, cognitive therapy and hypnotherapy.

Margaret Sutherland PhD was Head of Special Needs at a comprehensive school and has a research background in psychology. She has extensive experience in counselling and cognitive therapy.

Other jointly written books by the same authors:

*The Behaviour Management Toolkit*
*Strategies for Learning*

# Overcoming Common Problems Series

*Selected titles*

A full list of titles is available from Sheldon Press,
36 Causton Street, London SW1P 4ST, and on our website at
www.sheldonpress.co.uk

**The Assertiveness Handbook**
Mary Hartley

**Assertiveness: Step by Step**
Dr Windy Dryden and Daniel Constantinou

**Body Language: What You Need to Know**
David Cohen

**Breaking Free**
Carolyn Ainscough and Kay Toon

**Calm Down**
Paul Hauck

**The Candida Diet Book**
Karen Brody

**Cataract: What You Need to Know**
Mark Watts

**The Chronic Fatigue Healing Diet**
Christine Craggs-Hinton

**The Chronic Pain Diet Book**
Neville Shone

**Cider Vinegar**
Margaret Hills

**Comfort for Depression**
Janet Horwood

**The Complete Carer's Guide**
Bridget McCall

**The Confidence Book**
Gordon Lamont

**Confidence Works**
Gladeana McMahon

**Coping Successfully with Pain**
Neville Shone

**Coping Successfully with Panic Attacks**
Shirley Trickett

**Coping Successfully with Period Problems**
Mary-Claire Mason

**Coping Successfully with Prostate Cancer**
Dr Tom Smith

**Coping Successfully with Ulcerative Colitis**
Peter Cartwright

**Coping Successfully with Varicose Veins**
Christine Craggs-Hinton

**Coping Successfully with Your Hiatus Hernia**
Dr Tom Smith

**Coping Successfully with Your Irritable Bowel**
Rosemary Nicol

**Coping with Age-related Memory Loss**
Dr Tom Smith

**Coping with Alopecia**
Dr Nigel Hunt and Dr Sue McHale

**Coping with Blushing**
Dr Robert Edelmann

**Coping with Bowel Cancer**
Dr Tom Smith

**Coping with Brain Injury**
Maggie Rich

**Coping with Candida**
Shirley Trickett

**Coping with Chemotherapy**
Dr Terry Priestman

**Coping with Childhood Allergies**
Jill Eckersley

**Coping with Childhood Asthma**
Jill Eckersley

**Coping with Chronic Fatigue**
Trudie Chalder

**Coping with Coeliac Disease**
Karen Brody

**Coping with Compulsive Eating**
Ruth Searle

**Coping with Diabetes in Childhood and Adolescence**
Dr Philippa Kaye

**Coping with Diverticulitis**
Peter Cartwright

**Coping with Down's Syndrome**
Fiona Marshall

**Coping with Dyspraxia**
Jill Eckersley

# Overcoming Common Problems Series

**Coping with Eating Disorders and Body Image**
Christine Craggs-Hinton

**Coping with Family Stress**
Dr Peter Cheevers

**Coping with Gout**
Christine Craggs-Hinton

**Coping with Hay Fever**
Christine Craggs-Hinton

**Coping with Hearing Loss**
Christine Craggs-Hinton

**Coping with Heartburn and Reflux**
Dr Tom Smith

**Coping with Kidney Disease**
Dr Tom Smith

**Coping with Macular Degeneration**
Dr Patricia Gilbert

**Coping with the Menopause**
Janet Horwood

**Coping with a Mid-life Crisis**
Derek Milne

**Coping with Polycystic Ovary Syndrome**
Christine Craggs-Hinton

**Coping with Postnatal Depression**
Sandra L. Wheatley

**Coping with Radiotherapy**
Dr Terry Priestman

**Coping with SAD**
Fiona Marshall and Peter Cheevers

**Coping with Snoring and Sleep Apnoea**
Jill Eckersley

**Coping with a Stressed Nervous System**
Dr Kenneth Hambly and Alice Muir

**Coping with Strokes**
Dr Tom Smith

**Coping with Suicide**
Maggie Helen

**Coping with Tinnitus**
Christine Craggs-Hinton

**The Depression Diet Book**
Theresa Cheung

**Depression: Healing Emotional Distress**
Linda Hurcombe

**Depressive Illness**
Dr Tim Cantopher

**Eating for a Healthy Heart**
Robert Povey, Jacqui Morrell and Rachel Povey

**Every Woman's Guide to Digestive Health**
Jill Eckersley

**The Fertility Handbook**
Dr Philippa Kaye

**The Fibromyalgia Healing Diet**
Christine Craggs-Hinton

**Free Your Life from Fear**
Jenny Hare

**Free Yourself from Depression**
Colin and Margaret Sutherland

**Getting a Good Night's Sleep**
Fiona Johnston

**Heal the Hurt: How to Forgive and Move On**
Dr Ann Macaskill

**Help Your Child Get Fit Not Fat**
Jan Hurst and Sue Hubberstey

**Helping Children Cope with Anxiety**
Jill Eckersley

**Helping Children Cope with Change and Loss**
Rosemary Wells

**Helping Children Cope with Grief**
Rosemary Wells

**How to Approach Death**
Julia Tugendhat

**How to Be a Healthy Weight**
Philippa Pigache

**How to Beat Pain**
Christine Craggs-Hinton

**How to Cope with Difficult People**
Alan Houel and Christian Godefroy

**How to Get the Best from Your Doctor**
Dr Tom Smith

**How to Make Life Happen**
Gladeana McMahon

**How to Stop Worrying**
Dr Frank Tallis

**How to Talk to Your Child**
Penny Oates

**The IBS Healing Plan**
Theresa Cheung

**Is HRT Right for You?**
Dr Anne MacGregor

**Letting Go of Anxiety and Depression**
Dr Windy Dryden

**Living with Asperger Syndrome**
Dr Joan Gomez

# Overcoming Common Problems Series

**Living with Asthma**
Dr Robert Youngson

**Living with Autism**
Fiona Marshall

**Living with Birthmarks and Blemishes**
Gordon Lamont

**Living with Crohn's Disease**
Dr Joan Gomez

**Living with Eczema**
Jill Eckersley

**Living with Fibromyalgia**
Christine Craggs-Hinton

**Living with Food Intolerance**
Alex Gazzola

**Living with Grief**
Dr Tony Lake

**Living with Heart Failure**
Susan Elliot-Wright

**Living with Loss and Grief**
Julia Tugendhat

**Living with Lupus**
Philippa Pigache

**Living with Osteoarthritis**
Dr Patricia Gilbert

**Living with Osteoporosis**
Dr Joan Gomez

**Living with Rheumatoid Arthritis**
Philippa Pigache

**Living with Schizophrenia**
Dr Neel Burton and Dr Phil Davison

**Living with a Seriously Ill Child**
Dr Jan Aldridge

**Living with Sjögren's Syndrome**
Sue Dyson

**Losing a Baby**
Sarah Ewing

**Losing a Child**
Linda Hurcombe

**The Multiple Sclerosis Diet Book**
Tessa Buckley

**Overcoming Anorexia**
Professor J. Hubert Lacey, Christine Craggs-Hinton and Kate Robinson

**Overcoming Anxiety**
Dr Windy Dryden

**Overcoming Back Pain**
Dr Tom Smith

**Overcoming Depression**
Dr Windy Dryden and Sarah Opie

**Overcoming Emotional Abuse**
Susan Elliot-Wright

**Overcoming Hurt**
Dr Windy Dryden

**Overcoming Insomnia**
Susan Elliot-Wright

**Overcoming Jealousy**
Dr Windy Dryden

**Overcoming Procrastination**
Dr Windy Dryden

**Overcoming Shyness and Social Anxiety**
Ruth Searle

**The PMS Handbook**
Theresa Cheung

**Reducing Your Risk of Cancer**
Dr Terry Priestman

**The Self-Esteem Journal**
Alison Waines

**Simplify Your Life**
Naomi Saunders

**Stammering: Advice for all ages**
Renée Byrne and Louise Wright

**Stress-related Illness**
Dr Tim Cantopher

**Ten Steps to Positive Living**
Dr Windy Dryden

**Think Your Way to Happiness**
Dr Windy Dryden and Jack Gordon

**The Thinking Person's Guide to Happiness**
Ruth Searle

**Tranquillizers and Antidepressants: When to start them, how to stop**
Professor Malcolm Lader

**The Traveller's Good Health Guide**
Dr Ted Lankester

**Treating Arthritis Diet Book**
Margaret Hills

**Treating Arthritis – The Drug-Free Way**
Margaret Hills

**Treating Arthritis – More Drug-Free Ways**
Margaret Hills

**Understanding Obsessions and Compulsions**
Dr Frank Tallis

**When Someone You Love Has Depression**
Barbara Baker

Overcoming Common Problems

# Free Yourself from Depression

## Be your own therapist

COLIN SUTHERLAND BSc PhD

MARGARET SUTHERLAND MPhil PhD

sheldon PRESS

First published in Great Britain in 2008

Sheldon Press
36 Causton Street
London SW1P 4ST

The author and publisher have made every effort to ensure that the
external website and email addresses included in this book are correct and
up to date at the time of going to press. The author and publisher are not
responsible for the content, quality or continuing accessibility of the sites.

*British Library Cataloguing-in-Publication Data*
A catalogue record for this book is available from the British Library

ISBN 978–1–84709–041–6

1 3 5 7 9 10 8 6 4 2

Typeset by Fakenham Photosetting Ltd, Fakenham, Norfolk
Printed in Great Britain by Ashford Colour Press

Produced on paper from sustainable forests

# Contents

| | | |
|---|---|---|
| *Acknowledgements* | | xi |
| 1 | The five principles | 1 |
| 2 | The big picture | 7 |
| 3 | Control the way you think | 10 |
| 4 | Mind and body | 33 |
| 5 | Relationships | 53 |
| 6 | The power of language | 72 |
| 7 | Happiness | 79 |
| 8 | Sleep solutions | 90 |
| 9 | The big picture revisited | 95 |
| Appendix: Hypnotherapy tracks | | 105 |
| *Notes* | | 107 |
| *Bibliography* | | 109 |
| *Index* | | 111 |

*Note:* This is not a medical book and is not intended to replace advice from your doctor. Do consult your doctor if you are experiencing symptoms with which you feel you need help.

# Acknowledgements

In writing this book, we have discussed ideas and sought advice from many people. We would, however, like to thank and acknowledge the particular contributions made by Jonathan and Helen Allan, Vicky Brown and Dr Liz Newson for their helpful and constructive feedback.

# 1

## The five principles

This chapter includes:

- an overview of depression;
- an explanation of the five principles on which this book is based;
- an understanding of why the use of audio hypnotherapy sessions enhances behaviour change.

### Introduction

'Depression' is both an everyday word and a clinical term used to describe a particular set of symptoms ranging from a low mood state to more extreme mental and physical problems. This book is not a panacea for someone in a deep state of depression. But the techniques we teach can both assist recovery and help to stop depression recurring. Its approach is practical and forward-looking. It assumes you have experienced depression and wish to avoid it happening again. We want to help you to become mentally and physically strong enough to deal with things as they occur. We don't encourage you to delve into your past or ruminate on the causes of your depression. The past cannot be undone, but you can build a better future.

The strategies we will be teaching you are not difficult – in fact, some are so simple you'll wonder why you haven't tried them before. But remember, you can't take on everything at once. Changing behaviour takes time and practice, so work slowly on one or two things before moving on. Also remember, you're an individual. While some of the approaches will suit you, others may not, so have an open mind but also be selective.

If you have a close relationship with someone – a partner, parent, sibling or perhaps a friend – ask him or her to become involved and help you to make some of the changes. This involvement may even help to deepen your relationship.

Every experience we have changes us. We meet someone new and that meeting is registered in our brains by electrical activity and by chemical changes. When we practise something we develop new pathways in our brains. In this way, what was awkward and required thought becomes easier and easier and eventually becomes automatic. As you work through the exercises in this book and make changes, you will be changing your brain.

Clearly, it will be hard to alter those things that are most deeply ingrained. But big changes can be made. This is illustrated by our ability to change physical responses. For instance, in Britain people drive on the left-hand side of the road, and responses to this are automatic. But when British people go abroad, they soon adapt and learn to do the opposite. It may take a bit of effort, and at first it's easy to make mistakes, but with persistence, driving on the right becomes automatic. Similarly, with practice our psychological responses can be changed. At first you may find things a struggle and make mistakes, but if you stick with your changes eventually they will become part of you and will stop old behaviours recurring.

We are all different and so some things in this book will be more relevant to you and your situation than others. We suggest that you read through the whole book quite quickly and identify the sections that are most appropriate to you. When you have done this, you should go back and work through the areas identified and carry out the suggested exercises.

## The five principles

This is a practical book about depression. But good practice is based on a sound understanding of what really works. For this reason, all the practical activities that we suggest are based on five well-tested principles. These are:

1 We can control the way we think.
2 Good relationships are vital to our well-being.
3 The words we use affect our mood.

4 The mind–body relationship can be used to aid control of mood.

5 The imagination can be used in positive ways.

The notes below consider these in a little more detail. Read through them and think about each one before you go any further.

## 1 We can control the way we think

We all know that thinking has a powerful effect on mood. But are you aware of your power to control your own thoughts and feelings?

Back in the 1960s Aaron Beck, one of the co-founders of what is now called cognitive behaviour therapy (CBT), noticed that people with depression had very negative ways of thinking about themselves.[1] He went on to demonstrate that encouraging new and more positive ways of thinking could actually relieve the depression. Now, decades later, CBT has established itself as a key treatment for depression. Central to this sort of therapy is the idea of ANTs – not the ones we see in the garden, but the creepy crawlies of the mind. ANTs stands for Automatic Negative Thoughts, those pessimistic and unhelpful ways of thinking that affect us all but which can be particularly catastrophic to those who experience depression.[2]

Many of our ANTs are simply untrue or only partially true. So to deal with them we need to look at the evidence, and those that don't hold up to close scrutiny need challenging. If you can learn how to 'thought challenge' negative and harmful beliefs then you will have developed an important tool in fighting your depression. The notes and exercises in Chapter 3 will help you with this.

## 2 Good relationships are vital to our well-being

Having a range of good relationships with family, friends and colleagues is both a bulwark against depression and an aid to raising mood. When relationships are not good or fall apart, then the chances of going into depression are increased. So we encourage you to think about your own relationships, consider your skills in this area and make changes as necessary. Chapter 5 deals with this in detail.

## 3  The words we use affect our mood

Words, and how they are said, powerfully influence our thoughts, moods, feelings and actions. In his bestseller, *Blink*, science journalist Malcolm Gladwell recounts some language-priming experiments that have interesting outcomes for those involved in changing behaviour.[3] He describes how students were asked to unscramble sentences such as 'him about was worried she always'. Embedded in these sentences were words connected with old age, like 'old', 'lonely', 'wrinkled'. Before taking part in the experiment, and unbeknown to the students themselves, the time they took to walk down the long corridor to the experimenter's office was measured. It was then measured again after they had completed the test. Amazingly, on average the students' walk back from the office was significantly slower than their walk to the office, and a possible explanation is that their brains had adapted to suggestions of being old.

This is an example of what is known as a priming experiment. Many variations of this type of research have demonstrated the subtle effect that language can have on our feelings and the way we behave. While Chapter 6 looks specifically at this area, we have also tried to incorporate the idea into many of the other exercises and activities you will come across in the book.

## 4  The mind–body relationship can be used to aid control of mood

The mind–body interaction is a two-way process. It's easy to accept that the mind controls the body. We know that the brain controls movement, that when we feel nervous our hearts beat faster and that when we feel embarrassed our faces flush. But this is not the full story, because although the process is less obvious, the body also affects the mind. Next time you feel angry try this simple procedure, which will demonstrate the point: as your anger begins to build up, relax your muscles, breathe normally and smile. If you can do this you will notice your angry feelings subsiding.

By using muscle relaxation and breathing control, hypnotherapy employs the same sort of technique to create a calm, trancelike state of mind. Similarly, other therapies like meditation, massage and aromatherapy work in a comparable way. They also rely on muscle relaxation and/or slow deep breathing to quieten and soothe the mind. On the other hand, movement, muscle tension and breathing can be used, as necessary, to raise mood. Learning to use this mind–body relationship is an important tool in dealing with mood control.

Another aspect of mind–body interaction is the effect on feelings of what we eat and drink. Alcohol and caffeine are two obvious examples of this. Furthermore, both muscle relaxation and what we eat and drink affect our ability to go to sleep and the quality of sleep that we have.

Various aspects of the mind–body relationship are considered in Chapter 4, but the interaction between the two is also an important factor in many of the other areas discussed. Sleep is covered separately in Chapter 8.

### 5 The imagination can be used in positive ways

Imagination is a two-edged sword! By rehearsing things in our imagination we can prepare ourselves positively for future challenges. We can imagine facing a vital interview calmly; we can understand other people's feelings by 'putting ourselves in their shoes'; we can boost our confidence by seeing ourselves being successful. There are so many ways in which imagination can be a constructive and affirmative tool.

However, as those subject to depression know all too well, imagination also has its down side. Just as we can use imagination to support and encourage ourselves when challenged, we can also use it to 'catastrophize' – that is, to see a future made up only of problems and insurmountable difficulties.

Throughout this book, we will be encouraging you to use your imagination in positive ways and teaching you techniques that will counteract harmful ways of applying imagination.

### Hypnotherapy to back up behaviour change

Use of the imagination is enhanced during hypnosis, and we have prepared three audio hypnotherapy sessions that are available by free download from <www.behaviourchange.org> (for full details see the Appendix, p. 105). Regular use of these hypnotherapy sessions will act to augment and cement the behaviour changes being made. Research has recently shown that when cognitive behaviour therapy (CBT) is backed up by hypnotherapy there are greater improvements in mood than with CBT alone.[4] Furthermore, these improvements are more likely to be maintained.

# 2

# The big picture

This chapter will give you a chance to detail some of the good aspects of your life and identify where you have problems.

We all need to start from where we are at present. If we understand this, then change is possible.

The tables and boxes in this book are for guidance only and can be copied and used as a starting point, either as they are or adapted to your own particular purpose. Feel free to take a piece of paper and write as much as you like.

So begin by reviewing your own current situation. Make a start by thinking about the good things in your life and jot down your thoughts; Table 2.1 is a guide.

**Table 2.1 Good things**

| Area | Good things |
| --- | --- |
| Relationships | |
| Work | |
| Social life | |
| Hobbies | |
| Other things | |

Nobody's life is all plain sailing. We all encounter difficulties at some time. So now, identify some of your problem areas, as in Table 2.2.

**Table 2.2 Possible difficulties**

| Feelings | Causes | A problem for me? |
|---|---|---|
| Anxiety | Health | |
| | Going over things from the past | |
| | Worry about family | |
| | Relationship problems | |
| Loneliness | Retirement | |
| | Living alone | |
| | Bereavement | |
| | Divorce | |
| | Children leaving home | |
| | Working alone | |
| Perceived under-achievement | At work | |
| | At college | |
| | In relationships | |
| | In sport | |
| Relationships | Wanting a partner | |
| | Lack of friends | |
| | Breakdown of family relationship(s) | |
| | Work relationships | |
| Other areas | | |

---

**Box 2.1 Steve**

Steve is head of maths at a secondary school. He is finding the job more and more difficult. One of his staff is on long-term sick leave so he has had a succession of supply teachers to oversee. In addition, he has been having real difficulties in controlling one particular class and he is not coping with the amount of marking and administration he has to do. He is married with children who are still at school and he has a large mortgage. At home he works all evening and is losing touch with his family. He feels at the end of his tether and can see no way out.

---

In Box 2.1, Steve's problem at work is overwhelming him and he is at risk of sinking into depression.

It's not unusual for people to slip into depression because one particular issue seems to be insoluble. So, if you have a major problem that stands out from all the others, try to get it down on paper, using Box 2.2 as a guide.

---

**Box 2.2 My major problem at present is ...**

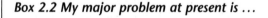

---

So you've reviewed your own situation, the good things as well as the problems. This is your starting point.

Now read on. The rest of this book will help you to decide on the changes that you want to make and how you can achieve them.

# 3

## Control the way you think

This chapter introduces you to cognitive behaviour therapy and some of its techniques. These include:

- challenging and changing thoughts;
- dealing with entrenched negative thoughts;
- preventing yourself from going over and over negative thoughts;
- getting a sense of proportion about things that go wrong;
- not playing the blame game;
- encouraging self-perception.

### Cognitive behaviour therapy (CBT)

In the 1960s, Albert Ellis and Aaron T. Beck independently put forward a thesis that was to have a powerful effect on the treatment of depression.[5] Their idea is encapsulated as follows:

> The way I think influences the way I feel, but I can change the way I think.

They had noticed a pattern of negative thinking in those they were treating for depression. It seemed that even those people who were clearly successful could, as a result of harmful ways of thinking, see themselves as failures. But they also recognized that it is possible for people to challenge and change their thoughts and, by doing this, to change the way that they feel. Other therapists began adopting this approach and now this apparently simple idea has become an established tool in combating depression.

Negative thinking tends to be the dominant mode of thought in people with depression. This leads to a high level of anxiety, a symptom that accompanies about 70 per cent of diagnosed cases of depression. However, it is also important to realize that there are limits to positive thinking. For instance, having the thought 'I'm strong, I can cope with anything' may sound good and make me perform really well, but there may come a time when I find myself in a situation with which I cannot cope.

If you've ever sought cognitive behaviour therapy for low mood or depression, you'll know that it can be difficult and expensive to obtain. So what we want to do here is teach you some of the techniques of 'thought challenging'. If you can successfully learn and utilize these, you'll be in a stronger position to deal with your own low moods in the future.

## Challenging and changing thoughts

We all talk to ourselves – it's a natural and normal thing to do. When you talk to yourself, this is called your 'inner voice'.

Sometimes you can hear your inner voice clearly but often you're hardly aware of it. Look at Tables 3.1 and 3.2, which give examples of the inner voice at work. Two different thoughts have been given for each situation. Look at how they affect the person's mood.

**Table 3.1 Jane's inner voice**

| Situation | |
|---|---|
| Jane rings her friend Sarah and suggests that they go to see a film. Sarah says she's got too much work to do at the moment. | |
| *Jane's thoughts* | *Mood* |
| **1** 'It's always like this. She probably finds me boring. I haven't really got any friends.' | Down |
| **2** 'That's a pity, but I know she's got her exams soon. I'll phone Sally and see what she's doing and if she doesn't want to go, I'll watch that new DVD I got yesterday.' | OK |

**Table 3.2 Adam's inner voice**

| Situation |
| --- |
| After a disastrous day at work, Adam has just arrived home. Sharon has been in all day, looking after their two young children. Adam just wants to talk about his day. Sharon wants him to play with the children. When he says he's too tired she accuses him of being a bad parent. |

| Adam's thoughts | Mood |
| --- | --- |
| 1 'The kids always come first. She's never interested in my problems.' | Down |
| 2 'Sharon needs a break and the first thing I do is moan about my day. I'll tell her about it when we've got the kids to bed.' | OK |

Things that have the potential to make us feel down happen all the time. Table 3.3 shows a few of them. See if you can come up with some of your own.

**Table 3.3 Things that can make us feel down**

Forgetting a list
Being late
Someone else being late
Losing keys
Getting a puncture
A task going wrong
Losing a parking space
Dropping something
Not being promoted
A disparaging comment

So life is full of hazards. Some are of our own making, some we can blame on others and some are just sheer bad luck. But how we feel and act on these is within our control and it starts with the way we think about them. The process is:

Thoughts ⟶ Feelings ⟶ Actions

In fact, the way you think about things has a profound effect on your whole life.

- It affects your relationships.
- It affects how you do things – whether, for instance, you persist or give up on something.
- It can make you angry or accepting, sad or happy.

But you don't have to accept negative thoughts. You can actually challenge and change the way you think about something. So let's start by helping you to develop an awareness of your own thinking. Table 3.4 is an example to get you going.

**Table 3.4 Anna's thinking**

| *Situation* | |
| --- | --- |
| Anna's boss points out a mistake she's made in writing up her monthly report. | |
| Negative thought | Positive thought |
| 'I'm always making mistakes. I'm useless at reports and he can't wait to put me down. I know he doesn't like me.' | 'I've made a bit of a mistake there, but he didn't comment about the rest of the report so that must be OK.' |
| Feeling ▼ | Feeling ▼ |
| Upset, pessimistic about the future, unappreciated. | OK. Ready to accept and correct the error and then move on in an optimistic way. |
| Actions ▼ | Actions ▼ |
| Shows she's upset. Can't get back into work mode. | Shrugs it away as a one-off mistake. Makes the changes and gets on with other things. |

Now get a piece of paper and, using the format in Table 3.5, describe some of the times you have thought negatively about a situation. When this is done, see if you can then come up with alternative, more positive thoughts for each circumstance. Follow these through by exploring how they would have affected your feelings and actions.

**Table 3.5 Challenging my thoughts**

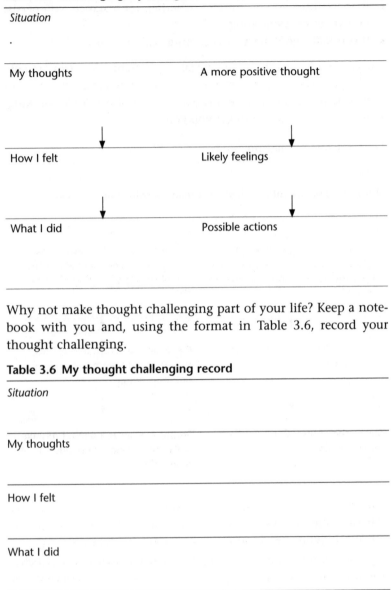

| Situation | |
| --- | --- |
| . | |
| My thoughts | A more positive thought |
| How I felt | Likely feelings |
| What I did | Possible actions |

Why not make thought challenging part of your life? Keep a notebook with you and, using the format in Table 3.6, record your thought challenging.

**Table 3.6 My thought challenging record**

*Situation*

My thoughts

How I felt

What I did

Some possible alternative thoughts

## Ways of dealing with ANTs

To get really good at thought challenging, you need to know a bit more about negative thoughts.

The same types of negative thought frequently occur in different circumstances, and they have a habit of creeping up on you. Aaron Beck[6] aptly called these:

**A**utomatic **N**egative **T**houghts

ANTs lurk around in your head and pop out as soon as something goes a bit wrong. Table 3.7 shows two examples of ANTs at work.

**Table 3.7 Two examples of ANTs at work**

| *Situation* | *Situation* |
| --- | --- |
| Johar has just bought some cupboards. As he puts them together, he misreads the instructions. He's now faced with the task of taking them all to pieces and starting again. | Sarah is a manager and needs to tell an employee that her work is not up to standard, a part of her job that she really dreads. She goes to tell the employee but then avoids the issue and talks about something else. |
| Johar's thought<br>'Oh no! It's all gone wrong.' | Sarah's thought<br>'I've ducked out again!' |
| Johar's ANTs<br>'This always happens to me. I'm just not practical. It's me, I'm useless.' | Sarah's ANTs<br>'I'm always such a coward. I'm just not up to the job. Everything in my life seems to go wrong.' |

Look at Sarah and Johar's language:

- 'This always happens.'
- 'It's me, I'm useless.'
- 'Everything in my life seems to go wrong.'

Can you see how small individual mistakes have been magnified and built into major problems?

There are three types of ANTs: ones that personalize problems, ones that make things permanent and ones that spread the gloom to all areas of life.

ANTs also tend to work together. That way the message they give can be more devastating. There's an example in Table 3.8.

### Table 3.8 ANTs working together

*Situation*
Jack's alarm doesn't go off. So he gets up late, misses his train and isn't on time for an important meeting.

Jack's thought
'I've blown it. We won't get that contract now.'

Jack's ANTs
'This sort of thing is *always* happening to *me. Every* time I think things are going well, *I* mess something up. *I* must be jinxed.'

As you can see, ANTs are destructive because they overwhelm you with gloom and demolish your hopes for the future. But the good news is that, by a very focused method of thought challenging, they can be defeated.

When things go wrong, we frequently believe the first thoughts that come into our heads. But initial thoughts can often be mistaken, so to start with we need to weigh up all the evidence. Table 3.9 is an example.

## Table 3.9 Alison weighs up the evidence

*Situation*
Paul and Anna are having a Christmas party and Alison has not been invited.

*Alison's first thoughts*

They just don't like me.

*Alison's feelings*
Upset and angry

### Challenges

*Evidence for*
No invitation

*Evidence against*
'Whenever we meet, they're always very friendly to me. In fact Paul helped me when my car wouldn't start last month and they did invite me to their barbecue last summer.'

*Other ways of looking at the problem*
'They've only got a small house and they've got all their family over, so they can't invite everyone. Perhaps it's just a close-friends-and-family do.'

'*Challenging my thoughts has made me feel better.* I'm not upset or angry now, just a bit disappointed. I've decided to stop thinking about their party and concentrate on what I am doing at Christmas.'

When you next have some ANTs to deal with, examine the evidence. Use the format in Table 3.10 to help you.

**Table 3.10 My situation: examining the evidence**

| Situation |
| --- |

| My first thoughts |
| --- |

| My feelings |
| --- |

| Challenge |
| --- |

| Evidence for |
| --- |

| Evidence against |
| --- |

| Other ways of looking at the problem |
| --- |

Challenging my thoughts has made me feel ...

I've decided to ...

A combination of thought challenging and measurement can also reduce the strength of the feelings that ANTs create. Box 3.1 shows how you do it, and Table 3.11 is an example of how it works.

---

**Box 3.1 Reducing the strength of negative feelings**

- Start by writing down your negative thoughts and the feelings these give you.
- Next, measure the strength of your feelings by giving them a number between 1 and 10.
- Then challenge your negative thoughts and replace them with more positive ones.
- Measure the strength of the feelings again.
- Challenge again with another positive thought and measure again.

Keep doing this until you have lowered the strength of your feelings.

---

### Table 3.11 Rob's thought challenges and measurements

*Situation*
Rob is a charge nurse who likes his job but hates all the paperwork he has to do. He feels very negative whenever he has to sit down to form-filling and writing up reports.

*Thoughts*
'I detest all this paperwork. It's so boring and repetitive. It takes up so much of my time. I came into this job to help people, not to be a form-filler.'

*Feelings*
Bored, miserable, gloomy.

*How strong are the negative feelings?*

| 1 | 2 | 3 | 4 | 5 | 6 | 7 | 8 | 9 | 10 |
|---|---|---|---|---|---|---|---|---|---|
| Weak | | | | Strong | | | | Very strong | |

*Thought challenging and measuring*
'I do enjoy the practical side of nursing. It's such a rewarding job. If I pace myself, I'll quickly get this lot out of the way.'

| 1 | 2 | 3 | 4 | 5 | 6 | 7 | 8 | 9 | 10 |
|---|---|---|---|---|---|---|---|---|---|
| Weak | | | | Strong | | | | Very strong | |

*Thought challenging and measuring*
'It will only take me an hour, and the rest of the day I'll be able to get on with the real job of helping patients.'

| 1 | 2 | 3 | 4 | 5 | 6 | 7 | 8 | 9 | 10 |
|---|---|---|---|---|---|---|---|---|---|
| Weak | | | | Strong | | | | Very strong | |

Copy the framework in Table 3.12, and use it to try out the measuring approach for yourself.

## Table 3.12 My thought challenges and measurements

*Thought*

---

*Feelings*

---

*How strong?*

| 1 | 2 | 3 | 4 | 5 | 6 | 7 | 8 | 9 | 10 |
|---|---|---|---|---|---|---|---|---|----|
| Weak | | | | Strong | | | | | Very strong |

*Challenging thought(s)*

---

*How strong are the feelings now?*

| 1 | 2 | 3 | 4 | 5 | 6 | 7 | 8 | 9 | 10 |
|---|---|---|---|---|---|---|---|---|----|
| Weak | | | | Strong | | | | | Very strong |

*Challenging thought(s)*

---

*How strong are the feelings now?*

| 1 | 2 | 3 | 4 | 5 | 6 | 7 | 8 | 9 | 10 |
|---|---|---|---|---|---|---|---|---|----|
| Weak | | | | Strong | | | | | Very strong |

*I feel OK now because ...*

---

## Preventing rumination

When you're feeling down, one gloomy thought can lead to
another, sometimes with disastrous results. Here's an example of
how a simple 'niggle' can build up, via negative thoughts, to a very
serious – and usually wildly inaccurate – conclusion.

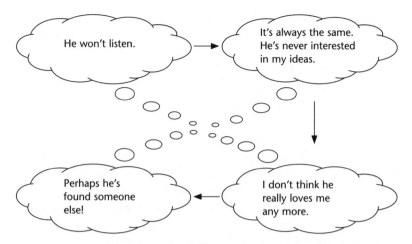

This is called ruminating. Cows are called ruminants because they chew over their food, swallow it, regurgitate it and chew it again. When used about humans, 'rumination' refers to the mind constantly 'chewing over' worrying thoughts.

Ruminating is one of the most dangerous forms of negative thinking. It is strongly associated with anxiety, anger and depression. The mood changes that accompany ruminating can relate to

---

### Box 3.2 How to stop ruminating

As soon as you become aware that you are ruminating, shout 'STOP' in a commanding way. Really put emphasis on the word. This can be done either silently or out loud.

Accompany the command with a small physical jolt – a pinch or a swift zap of an elastic band worn around your wrist.

Move yourself on, preferably to an activity that will absorb you so much that you can concentrate on nothing else. If that's not possible, move your mind on to other things like planning a holiday or some other pleasant activity.

Whatever you choose, accompany this change with taking a deep breath and, as you breathe out, relax the muscles of your stomach and shoulders and smile.

many things: the promotion you felt you deserved but didn't get, the time when you wished that you had behaved differently, the occasion when everything went wrong, the incident when you said the wrong thing, the episode when someone hurt you, and so forth. There are endless possibilities.

The important thing is to STOP ruminating. Box 3.2 shows you a way to do it.

Another difficulty with rumination is that you can be ruminating for a long time before becoming consciously aware of it. Practising the technique in Box 3.3 can help you with this particular problem. It will create in your mind an association between the feelings you get when ruminating and the need to stop and move yourself on.

---

### Box 3.3 Becoming aware that you are ruminating

Imagine a very large screen. On the screen, see yourself acting in a positive way, completely dissociated from ruminating. Now shrink this picture to the bottom right-hand side of the screen.

Go into your mind and think about how you feel when you ruminate ... Sad? Angry? Depressed ...?

Immediately you retrieve that feeling, very, very quickly grow the positive picture until it fills the screen again. Accompany this with a physical action like a sudden intake of breath or clenching of fists.

Relax, then repeat.

Do this mental exercise ten times on the first day, and then at least five times a day for the next week. Repeat in future as required.

---

## Weighing the evidence

Thought challenging is about being hopeful and confident in relation to the future, rather than just accepting a gloomy helplessness. So in that sense it's about being optimistic rather than pessimistic. But we are not suggesting that optimism is good and pessimism is bad. Most of us are a complex mixture of optimism and pessimism, and although generally it is better to view the future with hope and confidence, there are times when excessive optimism can be seriously misplaced.

However, continually adopting a pessimistic view of situations too often leads to a sense of being powerless to change things.

**Stenhouse Gallery**
require a
Senior Curator
35k + benefits

It's a great opportunity but I know they'd never consider me. I'm no good at interviews so it's not even worth me trying.

So when you do consider the evidence, try to weigh up the facts of the situation as accurately as possible. Assess both the positives and the negatives and then make your decision.

| +ve | I've got lots of experience. The exhibition last year was a great success. I am qualified for the job. | −ve | I am young for a senior position. I do get nervous at interviews. So far, they've always chosen men for the top jobs. |

When making decisions, get into the habit of weighing up the positive and negative facts of the situation but remember not to confuse ANTs with facts. The format in Table 3.13 may help you; copy it out and use it to weigh up the potential of situations.

**Table 3.13 Weighing up future situations**

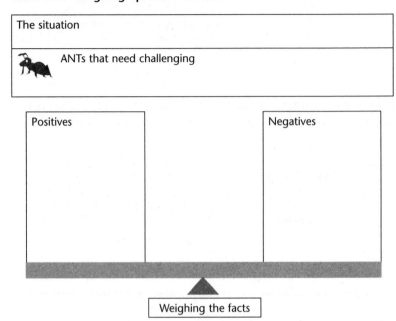

| The situation |
| ANTs that need challenging |

| Positives | Negatives |

Weighing the facts

## Getting a sense of proportion

'Catastrophizing' is when you look on temporary problems as a disaster, and as a result become totally demoralized about the future. It's a particularly malicious sort of ANT and requires a specific 'ANTidote' that goes like this:

1 Confront the worst thing that could happen and work out how you would cope with it. By doing this, you are not allowing yourself to become paralysed with fear and thus helpless in facing the future.
2 Think about what you really want to happen and how you can go about achieving this.

There's an example in Table 3.14.

**Table 3.14 Sanjay**

*This is the situation*
Sanjay wants to do computer science at Sheffield University. The university offers him a place as long as he gets two As and a B.
In his mock exams he gets a B and two Cs.

| *This is the worst thing that could happen* | *This is the best thing that could happen* |
| --- | --- |
| Not getting into Sheffield. | Achieving my grades and getting accepted by Sheffield. |
| *How would I cope with this?* Well, first, I know that this hasn't actually happened yet and I know that I have got time to get things right. But if I don't get into Sheffield next year, I could always try again the following year or I could look around for courses at other universities. Anyway, that's not a decision to make now. | *What I can do to help make the best thing happen* Ask my teachers to go over where I went wrong in the tests. Do some practice exams. Plan my revision. |

If you do find yourself catastrophizing, use this approach to help you think the situation through and move forward. Use the grid in Table 3.15 as a pattern to help you with this.

**Table 3.15 Thinking my situation through**

*The situation*

| This is the worst possible outcome | This is the best outcome |
| --- | --- |
| How would I deal with this? | To achieve the best outcome I need to |

Another sort of catastrophizing occurs when a problem seems just too big. There's an example of this in Box 3.4.

---

### Box 3.4 Amanda

Amanda is coming up to the end of her final year at university. She has a thesis to write. A couple of essays are still outstanding and she has several final exams to revise for. It's all getting too much for her. These are her thoughts:

'I'm never going to get through it all. I must finish the thesis otherwise I'll fail, but how will I have time to do revision and write those essays? I might as well give up.'

---

Of course, while she's panicking like this Amanda is not going to get anything done and this will make the problem even worse. It will become a vicious circle. Fortunately, Amanda's friend intervened. She convinced her not to lump the whole problem together, but just to recognize it as a series of manageable steps. That's the important lesson: however big the problem, you can break it down into manageable steps. So whenever you have to deal with something like this, use the process outlined in Table 3.16.

### Table 3.16 Breaking down the problem

| *This is the problem* |
| --- |
| |
| *Step 1 and when I will do it* |
| |
| *Step 2 and when I will do it* |
| |
| *Step 3 and when I will do it* |
| |
| *Step 4 and when I will do it* |
| |

## Not playing the blame game

Blaming is another area for consideration. When things go wrong, who or what do you tend to blame? Yourself? Other people? Bad luck? Circumstances? Obviously, at times it's reasonable to apportion blame. But with some people, blaming themselves or others for misfortunes becomes an automatic reaction rather than a thoughtful assessment of the facts, and this has a negative effect on their feelings.

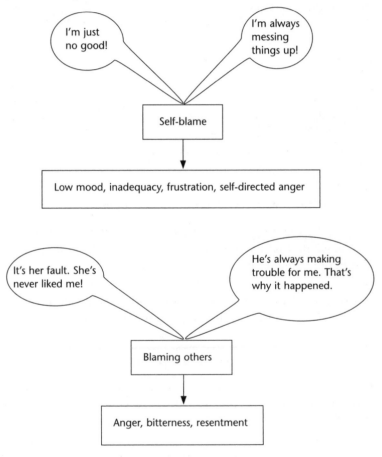

When things go wrong, too much self-blame will make you unnecessarily angry with yourself, while blaming others when it's not their fault will sour relationships.

Think about some recent things that haven't gone right for you. Who or what do you think was to blame for these problems? Use a grid like the one in Table 3.17 to help you work through the situation from this perspective.

**Table 3.17 Who or what was to blame?**

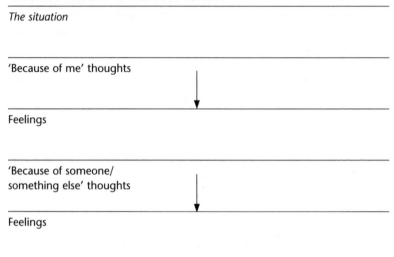

Suppose you changed your thoughts about who or what was to blame: would that have changed your feelings? Try this again with another problem. Can you see that who or what you blame for your problems also affects your feelings?

However, it may be a good idea to forget blame altogether and focus on how to prevent things going wrong in the future.

## Self-perception

In this chapter, we have tried to encourage you to think positively about things. But you do need to make sure that these positive thoughts don't just become mantras that disconnect you from the reality around you.

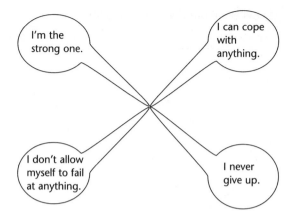

I'm the strong one.

I can cope with anything.

I don't allow myself to fail at anything.

I never give up.

Powerful thoughts like these can be useful in psyching yourself up to face a specific task, but they also can become too demanding and rigid. This is what happened to Jason (Box 3.5).

---

### Box 3.5 Jason

Jason was married with three children and had achieved his lifelong ambition of setting up his own business. He believed himself to be a strong person, a hard worker who could cope with anything. His business was successful and he was getting more and more orders and working longer and longer hours. He employed more staff but still couldn't seem to cope with the multiplicity of tasks. There were the accounts to do, the letters to write, the wages to sort out, customer complaints to deal with.

Things started to spiral out of control because he couldn't change that belief that he could cope with anything.

Fortunately his wife, Katie, challenged the damaging beliefs that Jason had about himself. She helped him to see that they weren't true and made him admit that he needed help.

She organized their friends and family to help him and his business through the crisis.

---

Think about how you view yourself.

Take a sheet of paper and try jotting down some of your beliefs about your own capabilities, using Table 3.18 as a guide. Do your beliefs need limiting in any way?

**Table 3.18 My beliefs about my own capabilities**

| Beliefs about my capabilities | What are the limits to these beliefs? |
| --- | --- |
| | |
| | |
| | |
| | |
| | |
| | |

## Recognize your own success

Although it's good to set yourself targets, some people set themselves impossible tasks and find it really difficult to recognize their actual successes. Andrew, in Box 3.6, is an example.

---

**Box 3.6 Andrew**

Andrew is a political journalist. He is greatly admired by his colleagues and his articles are so well written that they get published virtually unedited. He has regular columns in many of the top newspapers.

But Andrew himself is never satisfied with any of his articles. He always thinks he can do better. Even when people stop and congratulate him about a recent piece, he puts himself down. It's as if he can only see his under-achievements and never his achievements.

---

Andrew's way of thinking isn't that uncommon. It's actually surprising how many really successful people are over-critical of themselves in this way. It's as if they are always disappointed in themselves, and it's this constant feeling that they've let themselves down that can lead to depression.

Does this picture of Andrew strike a chord with you? Are you the sort of person who ignores success and always thinks you could improve on things? Are you always disappointed with the results, however much effort you put into things? If this is the case, then perhaps you need to change.

Perhaps you need to:

- scale down your targets;
- look more closely at things and recognize your actual accomplishments;
- learn to be less self-critical and more accepting of yourself;
- give yourself a pat on the back for successes, big and small.

If you do need to do some of these things, it will help you to jot them down in a grid like the one in Table 3.19.

**Table 3.19 Being less self-critical**

*How can I scale down my targets so they are more easily achievable?*

*How can I recognize and celebrate my achievements?*

*In what ways do I need to change my thinking?*

Reinforce the changes you are going to make by using the Stay in Control audio hypnotherapy track that you can download from <www.behaviourchange.org> (see p. 105).

Before using this track you will need to read through your thoughts on being self-critical, so that you can put them into operation in your imagination. This will really prepare you to follow through the change. Use the Stay in Control track in this way on a regular basis to achieve a permanent change.

## Summary

Remind yourself of the techniques in this section.

The way I think
influences the way I feel,

BUT

I can change the way I think.

In dealing with low mood, you need to understand and act on this message. Start now.

- Copy the practical worksheets so you have them ready whenever you need them.
- Get yourself a notebook to use for thought challenging and carry it around with you.
- Practise, practise, practise. Your happiness is dependent on being able to think positively.

Write the statement in the box above on to cards. Carry one around with you and place others in prominent positions where you will see them.

# 4

# Mind and body

This chapter focuses on the 'body to mind' process, and in doing this we will consider:

- the subtle ways we can use our bodies to control our mood and deal with unwanted emotions such as anger and anxiety;
- meditation and self-hypnosis;
- exercise;
- food.

## Introduction: the body–mind process

It's easy to accept that the mind controls the body but, except in the case of illness, the influence that the body has on the mind is less obvious. Nevertheless, there is an effect and this is particularly true in the area of emotions. As a simple test, try feeling angry at the same time as keeping your muscles relaxed, smiling and continuing to breath normally. In fact, many calming therapies, such as hypnotherapy, meditation, aromatherapy and visualization actually rely on the feedback that muscle relaxation and/or slow, deep breathing have on the brain.

But also, simple movements, muscle tension, breathing and facial expressions can be used to raise mood with immediate effect. Regular exercise can be used for long-term effects on mood.

Another area of mind–body interaction relates to food and drink. We all know how alcohol can affect mood. But eating habits such as binging can also do this. So can high consumption of certain types of food such as sugar, additives or those known to cause allergies.

## Deal with anger

Anger can be at a range of levels. Anger at injustices such as slavery or children in coalmines has led to great social advances in the world. Such anger is still appropriate today, whether the injustice is at a social level or at the level of an individual. Showing a child that you are angry at inappropriate behaviour is a way of conveying the seriousness of the misdemeanour.

However, in the dictionary, anger is also defined with words like 'rage' and 'wrath', which infer that things are out of control. With the possible exception of a life-threatening situation, this type of anger is not an appropriate response to a situation. It doesn't help to resolve things and is generally unpleasant for those involved. This type of anger can also provoke a similar reaction from another individual or create fear, both of which can destroy a relationship.

If you are the sort of person who easily becomes angry, you don't have to accept the situation. You can, if you choose, do something about it. But to do this you must be prepared to learn three things. You need to learn how to:

- recognize the type of situation that causes you to feel angry (don't forget to include drinking alcohol if that applies);
- modify your angry thoughts and, if appropriate, take action to deal with the situation that has provoked your anger;
- counteract the physical effects of anger.

If you do easily lose your temper and want to make some changes, start by recognizing the things that make you angry. Take some paper and make a list of your thoughts, as in Box 4.1.

---

*Box 4.1  What makes me angry?*

I get angry when:

- 
- 
- 
- 

---

Anger is triggered by the way that you think about a situation – in other words, it actually starts in the brain. Unfortunately, when you are angry, rational thought goes out of the window. You are sure you are right. It's only when you have calmed down that you can really see the situation for what it is. Regrettably, that can sometimes be too late. Hurtful things are said, people are offended and it can take a long time to put things right.

The good news is that just as thoughts trigger anger, so you can use your thoughts to counteract its effect. This, if you remember, is called 'thought challenging'. We covered this process in Chapter 2, but there is another example in Box 4.2.

---

### Box 4.2 Neil's thought challenging

Neil has a teenage son, Ed, who stays in bed until all hours. He leaves the bathroom in a mess, doesn't clear up his own room and tries to avoid helping around the house. He's a typical teenager, but Neil finds this difficult to deal with. He broods on Ed's behaviour and gets angrier and angrier about it. Neil often flies into a rage when he remonstrates with Ed. This spoils the atmosphere in the home, not just for Neil and Ed but for everyone else as well.

Neil decides things can't go on like this, so he decides to challenge the way he's been thinking about the situation. He replaces his angry thoughts with these:

- 'It is common for teenagers to behave in this way.'
- 'I was probably like that myself.'
- 'What does it matter if he stays in bed?'
- 'It's unacceptable that he is so untidy and doesn't help around the house, so we do need to talk.'
- 'I'll choose a good time to have a serious talk with him about this. If necessary I'll discuss sanctions with Elaine.'

Challenging his thoughts this way stops the rumination. He's still annoyed, but not angry. Neil feels a lot happier because he feels that he has taken control of the situation.

---

Anger has obvious physical effects. When you are angry a whole range of changes occur in your body.

- Your pupils dilate.
- Your heart beats faster.
- Adrenaline is released into your bloodstream.
- Your blood is shunted preferentially to your muscles.
- Your breathing quickens but at the same time becomes shallower.
- Your muscles tense up and you particularly feel this in your stomach, shoulders and jaw.
- Your face distorts into a scowl.

But just as certain bodily changes strengthen rising anger, so alternative bodily changes can decrease it.

Some people will suggest that you should let your anger out by doing physically aggressive things like using a punch-bag. If anger is already established then some form of physical activity may be useful in burning it off, but it does not have to be aggressive. How about going for a run, taking a cycle ride or mowing the lawn? But be careful: anger makes you more prone to accidents so don't drive, and take care if you choose to run or cycle.

A better way is not to let the anger become established in the first place. When you feel yourself getting angry, we suggest that you actually use your body to counteract it.

From the list of physical effects, there are three things that you can really change. These are your breathing, your muscle tension and your facial expression.

Become sensitive to the situations that make you angry and then take action. Challenge your angry thoughts. Slow down your

---

### Box 4.3 Managing anger

*Change* your breathing by breathing deeply, but slowly. It is important that you breathe out for longer than you breathe in. Counting to four as you breathe in and six as you breathe out will help this process.

*Relax* your muscles. In particular, pay attention to the muscles in your stomach, shoulders and jaw but include all areas of the body. Concentrate on each area in turn and consciously tell those areas to relax. It can be useful to combine the relaxation of each muscle group with the act of breathing out.

*Slacken* your facial muscles and smile.

breathing. Relax your muscles. Smile. Combining these will help to neutralize your anger.

Next time you feel yourself getting angry, try the method outlined in Box 4.3.

The Stay in Control audio hypnotherapy track that you can download from <www.behaviourchange.org> will help you to develop this strategy. If you know that something is likely to make you angry, try using this track before it happens. This will allow you to rehearse how you wish to behave, while feeling calm and in control. For full instructions see the Appendix, p. 105.

## Deal with anxiety

Anxiety has been shown to accompany most cases of clinical depression and in many cases it is thought to be the cause. It is draining both to the individuals who experience it and to those around them. But, just as you can decide to reduce your anger, you can choose to lower your levels of anxiety. In fact, there is some similarity in the way that you deal with both problems.

Boxes 4.4 and 4.5 illustrate different types of anxiety.

---

### Box 4.4 Sheila's anxiety

Sheila has recently retired, having had a very busy life juggling work and family. She has two daughters and four grandchildren, all of whom live close by. She has always been a bit of a worrier but now she finds that she worries over her grandchildren's behaviour and their school progress, her children's relationships with their partners, her husband's health, and so on. When her daughters dismiss her anxieties she takes offence and ruminates on that.

---

### Box 4.5 Mark's anxiety

Mark hasn't got a job. He left his last job at a factory because he felt intimidated by the foreman under whom he worked. His doctor initially diagnosed stress, so he got security benefits, but he is now under pressure to get another job. Just the thought of going for an interview and then starting work again causes a very high level of anxiety. He has similar anxieties about socializing with people of his own age. He spends most of his time on his allotment where he can talk to mainly older men about growing things.

Sheila is a worrier and ruminator, whereas Mark's anxiety is provoked by fear.

The solution for Sheila could be a mixture of things.

- She could find something that absorbs her as her work used to do. For example, she might decide to become involved in an organization like the University of the Third Age (U3A), do voluntary work, go to an evening class or take up a hobby.
- She could challenge her thoughts.
- She could learn to relax more by meditating or using the Stay in Control hypnotherapy track (see p. 105).
- She could take regular exercise. For example, she could join a rambling, Tai Chi or yoga group. This could also add another social dimension to her life.

If you, like Sheila, are a regular ruminator, make a list of the things you could do.

Mark's needs are different. He needs to confront his fears, and to do this he should start with the situations that create the least anxiety. If your problems are more like Mark's, list the things that create anxiety for you; Table 4.1 is a guide. Then, according to how anxious you are in each particular situation, give each one a score of between one and ten, with ten being the highest level of anxiety.

**Table 4.1 My anxieties**

| Situation | Anxiety score |
| --- | --- |
|  |  |
|  |  |
|  |  |
|  |  |

When it is convenient for you, choose a situation that creates the smallest level of anxiety. Set up your audio player in a quiet room. Sit in a comfortable chair and play the Confronting Fears track (downloadable from <www.behaviourchange.org>, see the Appendix, p. 105). This will enable you to rehearse facing a situation that causes anxiety, while feeling calm and in control.

As soon as possible after using the track you should then confront that situation in reality.

Repeat this process with the other anxieties that you have identified. With situations that cause a high level of anxiety, use the Confronting Fears track on several consecutive days before facing that situation. This will help you to reduce your anxiety levels before confronting the fear.

In physical terms our responses to anxiety are similar to those produced by anger. Breathing again gets faster but shallower, and muscles tense up. So to manage anxiety you should follow a similar process to the one you used for dealing with anger, as in Box 4.6.

---

**Box 4.6 Managing anxiety**

- Count to four as you breathe in and six as you breathe out, exhaling for longer than you inhale.
- As you slowly breathe out, relax your muscles. Focus in particular on the muscles of your shoulders and your stomach.
- Slacken your facial muscles, particularly those around your eyes and your forehead.
- Smile.

---

## Smile! It makes you feel good

When describing how to deal with both anger and anxiety, we suggested smiling. Everyone knows the old adage 'Smiling makes you feel good' but is there any evidence for it? Well, yes, there is. It comes from the work of two psychologists, Paul Ekman and Wallace Friesen, who studied in detail how expressions are created by the muscles in the face.[7] As part of their research they decided to practise different expressions. They found that even just practising them affected how they felt. Using volunteers, they then set up a series of controlled experiments that confirmed the finding that facial expressions affect mood.

The conclusion from all this is that the expression you wear on your face reinforces the mood that the expression represents. What does this mean in practical terms? Well, we all know that we can, and often do, change our expressions. So if you're feeling down, one way of counteracting this mood is to change your expression.

Test this out for yourself. Start your day by smiling at yourself in the mirror when you're washing, shaving, putting on makeup, combing your hair, or whatever. Smile as you say good morning to others in your home and at work. Deliberately smile as you drive to work or purchase your bus or train ticket. Get into the habit of smiling even when you don't feel like it. Remember that the muscles involved in smiling are feeding back information to your brain and counteracting low mood.

Another thing to remember about smiling is that it's infectious. Try it for yourself. Smile at someone and almost inevitably that person will smile back at you.

Smiling and laughter are facilities lost during depression but they can be used to help stop it recurring.

## Avoid highs and lows

Some people, and perhaps you're one of them, live their lives on highs and lows.

The high is great. It's a time when you connect with the world, a time of great industry and achievement, a time when you are at your most creative and successful. However, it's unusual to live at this pitch all the time. Both the mind and the body need periods of stability and calmness to recover and regain the energy that is expended during a high. And, for some people, this is where the problem lies. They can't simply return to a slower and steadier pace of life and they actually pay for the high. They swing too far the other way and enter a low.

If you live on highs and lows, you'll undoubtedly know that a low can be a very deep trough indeed and can be extremely difficult to escape from. So how should you deal with it? In order to avoid the lows it's actually necessary to avoid the highs. The Stay in Control hypnotherapy track (see the Appendix, p. 105) will help you to maintain a more even keel. Listen to this track every day, more than once if necessary. It takes just 15 minutes and will enable you to focus your mind on staying calm and relaxed.

You'll find that a relaxed mind can still be productive and creative. And while you may not get things done as fast as when you're on a high, you can keep going at that slower pace for much longer without losing your momentum.

If you prefer it, you can also use meditation to engender feelings of peace and calm and prevent yourself from going into an unsustainable high.

Whichever technique you decide to adopt, make it part of your daily routine. Don't wait for a high before you start.

## Change your posture

When you are sad or depressed, you really do 'look down'.

- Your head bends forward and your eyes tend to look towards the ground.
- Your mouth turns down at the corners.
- Your shoulders are hunched.
- A depressed person even walks more slowly!

Just as facial expressions reinforce mood, so does posture and the way you move. And the solution is the same. Just as you can change your expression, you can also change the posture of your whole body.

So next time you start to feel low, use your entire body to challenge your feelings.

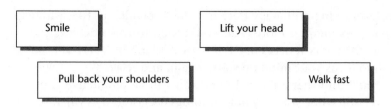

## Energize yourself

When you're feeling a bit low it can be very difficult to motivate yourself to do anything. So here is a routine that you can use to get yourself going.

### Step 1

Tell yourself how great it'll feel when you've got the thing done. Say it out loud and really mean it.

### Step 2

Use your imagination. In your mind really see all the benefits of having got the job done.

### Step 3

Imagine how you'll feel when this task isn't hanging over you. Relieved? Happy? And …?

## Step 4

Energize yourself:

- Stand up straight, hold your head high, pull your shoulders back.
- Tense your muscles – stomach, shoulders, arms, hands.
- Relax your muscles.
- Repeat this three times.

## Step 5

Start the task immediately.

### Take a pride in how you look

We all enjoy getting comments like these. But when you are feeling low, it's often hard to make an effort with your appearance. It seems to require energy, and that is in short supply. The trouble is, if you do give up on how you look, you not only miss out on the positive remarks, you also provoke disparaging comments and looks that make you feel even worse.

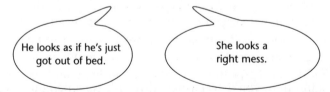

So however you feel, make an effort and, as with everything else we've discussed in this chapter, you'll discover that even the process of doing this can improve your mood. Work on your appearance as part of your daily routine and don't go out without freshening up and putting on something you feel good in.

For special occasions, treat yourself. Buy yourself something new to wear, have a relaxing massage or get your hair done. Say to yourself:

Look good $\longrightarrow$ Feel better

## Try meditation and self-hypnosis

In many ways, meditation and hypnosis are similar. They both encourage relaxation but in subtle ways they increase your energy. Which one you prefer using depends on personal taste, but they both have an important contribution to make. They can help you to unwind, manage unwanted emotions such as anxiety and deal with the people and events in your life.

### Meditation

The word 'meditation' can conjure up visions of elderly gurus sitting cross-legged, and for many people it does link into their spiritual and religious lives. However, it is no longer restricted to those realms and is now commonly used by people to keep a sense of peace and calm in their lives. Many people who meditate regularly also maintain that it helps them to become more focused on tasks and improves their relationships with others.

There are many different types of meditation but we will detail just one, which is perhaps the simplest and most widely used. It is called 'Mindfulness' and focuses on breathing.

- Choose a quiet place without distractions. The time of the day must obviously suit your activities, but if you meditate early in the day it will set you up for whatever lies ahead.
- Meditation stools and cushions are available commercially, but an ordinary upright chair is fine. If you do use a chair, you may find that it helps to tilt it forward a little by putting something under the back legs. Alternatively, you could sit on the sort of wedge-shaped cushion commonly available for office chairs.
- We will assume that you are sitting on a chair. Try not to slouch.

It is preferable to have your back straight but not rigid. Uncross your legs and have your feet flat and firmly on the floor. Sit a little forward so that your back does not touch the chair. Allow your hands to rest on your lap so that they are supported.

- When you are sitting comfortably just close your eyes, feel a general sense of relaxation and take a couple of slow deep breaths.
- Then allow your mind to be aware of your breathing. Breathe in and out through your nose if possible, or in through your nose and out through your mouth.
- Any time that your mind wanders away and you become aware that this has happened, just bring it back to awareness of your breathing. Do this in a relaxed way. This is not an exercise in concentration.
- If thoughts crop up then just accept them and move your mind back to your breathing.

The normal length of a meditation session is between 10 and 20 minutes, though it can be longer if you wish. One or two sessions each day can make a big difference to how you feel and perform.

If you find this difficult to practise on your own, joining a meditation group could help.

Meditation is also an important aspect of some kinds of yoga, so you might like to practise both exercise and meditation by joining a yoga group.

### Self-hypnosis

You can also obtain a 'peaceful purposefulness' by practising self-hypnosis. To start with, find a quiet place where you can sit comfortably. Sit down and close your eyes. Then focus your mind on your body.

- Notice the pressure of your body against the chair.
- Become aware of the pressure of your lips against each other.
- Notice the cooling sensations around your nostrils as you breathe in.
- Focus your mind on the sensations in the tips of your fingers.
- Slowly take a deep breath, and as you breathe out relax the muscles of your head and neck.

- Take another slow deep breath, and as you breathe out relax your shoulders, arms and hands.
- Take a third slow deep breath, and as you breathe out relax your back, chest and stomach muscles.
- Take a fourth slow deep breath, and as you breathe out relax the muscles controlling your hips, legs and feet.
- Take a fifth slow deep breath, and as you breathe out let any remaining tension go.

Finally, choose a place from your memory that is both beautiful and peaceful – a place where you feel safe and secure. It could be a beautiful garden, a waterfall, a beach or your own home. Go there in your imagination and open yourself up to that peace and beauty, allowing it to flow into you from all around. Then, when you feel rested and calm, just leave that beautiful, peaceful place, count up to five and be awake to the world with your conscious mind back in control.

## Exercise regularly

In 1994, the *British Medical Journal* published a major review of the research carried out on the effects of exercise on mood. It concluded that 'exercise boosted self-esteem, reduced mild anxiety and depression, favourably influenced mood and calmed down stress related conditions'.[8]

Recent studies show that an aerobic workout can make you feel revitalized and energized for hours. Moreover, you'll find that if you exercise regularly you'll not only raise your general level of fitness but you'll have more energy even on days when you haven't been able to work out. Regular exercise has also been shown to improve the quality of sleep.

So for anyone prone to depression, exercise is a must.

If you haven't exercised much for a long time, remember that it's important to build up the level and duration of exercise gradually. Your local leisure centre will normally do a fitness assessment and advise you. But remember, the less exercise interrupts your life, the more you will keep it up.

Try to:

- use the stairs rather than a lift or an escalator;
- walk or cycle short distances rather than using the car or the bus;
- walk or cycle to work if that is possible.

Make time for a few minutes of exercise at the start of the day. This is the optimum time for raising your mood.

- To keep supple, begin with some simple stretching exercises using your neck, shoulders, arms, waist, hips, legs and feet.
- Then follow this up with something aerobic, like running up and down the stairs a few times. This will get your blood flowing faster. You'll feel more alert and energized after this.

### Get someone else involved

If you make an arrangement to go to the gym or attend a keep-fit class with someone else, you're far more likely to keep it up.

### Take up a sport

You'll persevere with exercise if you find it fun. So try taking up a sport. How about

- badminton
- table tennis
- tennis
- football
- cycling
- walking
- swimming
- yoga
- ???

Look in at your local leisure centre to see what's on offer.

## You are what you eat – you can't be anything else

Another important area where mind and body interact relates to food and drink consumption. Human beings have known about the mood-changing effects of alcohol for thousands of years. But more recently we have come to recognize that individuals may have sensitivities to a whole range of foods and that these can have both physical and mental effects.

In 2000, the mental health charity MIND commissioned a study on food and mood.[9] This reported that, for some people suffering from depressive symptoms, changes in diet can and do affect mood.

Problems can occur because certain foods cause allergies. These don't necessarily show themselves in obvious ways such as the occurrence of skin rashes or other clear physical symptoms. Instead, they cause a mood depression. For those to whom this applies, cutting out the troublesome food can be life-enhancing. However, it is important to stress that food sensitivity is only a factor for some people suffering from depression or low mood. But if you are experiencing low mood, it's worth experimenting with your diet to see if what you eat contributes to your feelings.

So which foods are likely to be the culprits?

The most commonly implicated foods are wheat and dairy products. Other foods identified as possible culprits include oranges, yeast, tomatoes, corn and soy. If you do consume a lot of any of these foods, it could be worthwhile cutting out one or other of them for a few weeks while keeping a log of your mood. Table 4.2 shows a good way of doing this.

**Table 4.2 Food and mood**

| The food I am cutting out is | My mood – scale 1 to 10 1 = very low; 10 = great |
| --- | --- |
| Week 1 | |
| Week 2 | |
| Week 3 | |
| Week 4 | |

If a particular food has a clear effect, it could be time to make a permanent change to your diet.

## Additives

MIND also reported that foods containing high levels of additives are best avoided.

So check the additives in any processed foods that you consume on a regular basis. If they do contain a lot of additives, either look for a brand without the additives or experiment by cutting out these foods.

Similarly, look carefully at your consumption of sugary foods, stimulants like tea and coffee and obvious mood changers such as alcohol.

With each in turn, use your 'food and mood' record to investigate whether abstinence improves your mood.

## Essential fatty acids

Low levels of essential fatty acids (EFAs) have been associated with depression, and treatment with supplements has shown positive results in initial studies.[10] These EFAs are found in nuts, seeds and oily fish. A reduction in anxiety following treatment with EFAs has also been shown,[11] so why not try eating nuts, seeds and oily fish, or take a supplement?

## Comfort eating

When people are depressed, it's not unusual for them to seek solace in food. The problem is that eating too much can lead to weight gain, with a consequent lack of self-esteem that further depresses mood. Thus overeating and feeling depressed becomes a vicious circle.

Overweight people often have a habit of bingeing on foods that are very rapidly broken down to glucose.

- A rapid rise in blood glucose causes a similar rapid rise in blood insulin.
- This rapid rise in insulin then results in a fast drop in blood glucose, causing it to drop below baseline level.
- The result is that feelings of hunger are again stimulated.

This cycle of bingeing and quickly feeling hungry again adds to the feelings of low esteem and low mood.

Foods have now been categorized according to how fast they cause a rise in blood glucose. This is called the Glycaemic Index (GI) and information is available in many modern diet books.

If you have got into the habit of bingeing on rapidly absorbed carbohydrates, then here is a programme for you to try.

- Avoid soft drinks, pure fruit juice, potatoes, white rice, white bread, cakes and biscuits made with refined flour. They all cause

**Table 4.3  A week's eating and drinking**

| | *What I ate and drank* |
| --- | --- |
| Monday | |
| Tuesday | |
| Wednesday | |
| Thursday | |
| Friday | |
| Saturday | |
| Sunday | |

a rapid rise in blood glucose, and this is particularly intensified when they are eaten without other food.

- If you find it difficult to limit your carbohydrate intake, try alternatives such as granary bread, brown rice, and cakes and biscuits made with wholemeal flour. The fibre in these slows down the digestion process and consequently the rises in blood glucose are slow.
- Eat potatoes with other vegetables containing plenty of fibre.
- Eat the whole fruit rather than drinking fruit juices.
- Choose to eat foods with a low Glycaemic Index score.

But it's not just a case of cutting back on things that are bad for you. Feeling fit and well stems from a range of things, one of which

**Table 4.4 Types of food consumed**

| Type of food | My weekly consumption |
|---|---|
| Wheat | |
| Milk and cheese | |
| Refined carbohydrates and potatoes | |
| Soft drinks and fruit juices | |
| Stimulants, e.g. coffee, chocolate | |
| Oily fish | |
| Alcohol | |
| Changes I'm going to make | |

is having a good healthy diet rich in fruit, vegetables, grains, nuts and seeds.

Analyse your own food and drink consumption over a typical week and decide on any changes that you want to make; record this in an easy-to-read way, like Tables 4.3 and 4.4.

In this chapter, we have asked you to consider various ways in which the body can affect the mind. Obviously, not everything that we have suggested is going to be applicable to your particular situation. But some things will be, so take time out to think about our ideas and decide whether you want to take some of them on board.

# 5

# Relationships

In this chapter you will briefly analyse your own relationships. It also introduces you to various relationship skills. Obviously, only some may be relevant to your situation, but they include:

- being a good listener;
- being sensitive to others;
- not sulking;
- being open to criticism;
- learning how to resolve conflicts;
- improving your body language;
- learning to say 'no' when necessary.

## Introduction and self-analysis

Human beings are social animals, and when things go wrong in our relationships the results can be devastating. For this reason, problem relationships are often a major cause of depression. But the reverse is also true. An understanding partner, a good friend or a strong bond with a son or daughter or parent can act as a solid buffer against negative thinking and its consequences.

We hope that this chapter will help you to think about your own relationships, to consider whether changes are needed and, if so, how these can be achieved. In doing this, it's important to remember that the only behaviour you can actually change is your own. Nevertheless, any changes you do make may well have positive effects on those around you. If other people begin to view you differently, it's likely that their behaviour will also begin to change.

Relationships are complex, so we won't be able to cover everything. Our aim here is to lay down a few useful strategies for you to try out. If this doesn't help you with your particular relationship problems then perhaps you need the more personalized approach of a counsellor. We would suggest that this should be someone who specializes in Interpersonal Therapy or Cognitive Behavioural Therapy (CBT). Research has shown these to be the most effective psychological treatments for depression.

If you do decide to make some changes, don't try and do everything at once. Make small changes and stick to them. Allow them to become part of you before moving on to other things. Trying a complete makeover in one go rarely works.

To get started on this section, it would be useful to make some assessment of the important relationships in your life. Are you completely satisfied with them? Do you want to improve some aspects? If so, have you any ideas on how to do this?

So to start off, detail the relationships that are important to you. Then describe what, if anything, needs improving. Jot it down, as in Table 5.1.

**Table 5.1 Relationships that matter to me**

| Relationship | Comments |
|---|---|
|  |  |
|  |  |
|  |  |
|  |  |

Good relationships rely on particular skills. Think about the skills that you bring to your relationships. Then take some paper and use the headings in Table 5.2 to help you to make some notes on how you handle your relationships.

**Table 5.2 How I handle relationships**

| Me | Comments |
|---|---|
| Am I a good listener? | |
| Am I open about my feelings and ready to discuss problems? | |
| Am I sensitive to other people's needs? | |
| Do I sometimes resort to sulking? | |
| Can I handle criticism? | |
| Can I control my anger? | |
| Is my body language OK? | |

Developing these skills is the subject of this chapter, with the exception of anger, which has been covered in Chapter 4.

We all know that good intentions are not enough. Making a decision to improve your relationship skills is a start. But to ensure this really works, you need to monitor and reassess your progress on a regular basis. To help you do this, we suggest that you make some copies of Table 5.3. Then, using a separate sheet for each skill, you can track your progress every few days.

**Table 5.3 Skill progress check**

*Skill*

| Date | Observations |
| --- | --- |
|  |  |
|  |  |
|  |  |
|  |  |
|  |  |

## Learn to listen

Have you ever had a conversation like this? If you have, you'll know the difference between listening and hearing. You'll know that when someone really listens to you, he or she shows interest and involvement in what you're saying. Demonstrating that you can reproduce what has just been said is not listening.

Being a good listener may not come naturally to you. But it is something you can learn to do and it's worth it, because listening is a vital social skill. It shows that you are interested in others, in their thoughts and opinions, and are concerned about their lives. Listening actually cements relationships.

So where do you start?

Well, you first need to learn to hold back and let others actually have their say. You may have a lot to say on the subject. You may fiercely disagree with the speaker. He or she may have said it all before. But hang on, hear the speaker out, and when you do speak don't just launch into your own contribution but try to respond to what has been said. Summarize and ask questions before giving your own views. In that way you've demonstrated that you have actually listened. Don't get involved in conversations like this:

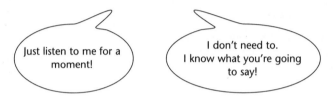

> Just listen to me for a moment!

> I don't need to. I know what you're going to say!

Showing that you are listening actually involves your whole body, and there are several ways you can do this. Look at Box 5.1.

---

### Box 5.1 Showing that you are listening

#### Make eye contact

The right level of eye contact is important in any relationship. Staring into the distance in an unfocused way makes it clear that you're thinking of other things, but too much eye contact can also be disconcerting. So relax and get a level of eye contact that makes you feel comfortable.

#### Use your face

Nod, smile, look sympathetic, show concern or whatever is appropriate for the situation.

#### Show that you are receptive

Uncross your arms and legs and also lean very slightly towards the speaker.

#### Keep still

Fidgeting will make you seem impatient.

But remember, body language is a subtle thing and we're all very quick to pick up on insincerity. So, if you decide to adopt any changes, only make the ones with which you can genuinely feel comfortable.

It's now time to review your own listening skills and decide if you want to make any changes. Put them down on paper, as in Table 5.4.

**Table 5.4 Becoming a better listener**

| Am I a good listener? | Action I need to take |
| --- | --- |
| Do I give others the opportunity to talk and do I encourage them to do so? | |
| When someone is talking, do I keep focused on him or her with my eyes and facial expressions? | |
| Do I keep my body language open and receptive? | |
| Am I patient or do I keep interrupting? | |
| Do I encourage the person who is talking by asking questions? | |
| Do I show sympathy and understanding in my responses? | |

## Be sensitive

Many relationships run into trouble because one person is insensitive to the needs, moods and interests of the other. Box 5.2 gives an example.

---

**Box 5.2 Gareth and Fiona**

Gareth and Fiona are partners. Gareth works for a company as a toolmaker while Fiona works at home designing internet web pages. Gareth socializes a lot during the day. He also plays football for his works team, which requires a couple of training sessions a week in addition to a match on Sunday mornings. He feels his life is so full he doesn't want to do anything else and when he is at home he becomes glued to the television, particularly when sport is on. Fiona feels more and more resentful and accuses Gareth of being selfish and insensitive, which he undoubtedly is, even though he loves Fiona in his own way.

---

Are you sensitive to the needs of the people close to you? Or do you always put your own interests first, like Gareth?

Being sensitive means showing concern. Fiona would have felt a lot less resentful if Gareth didn't immediately switch on the television but took time out to find out about her day and how she was feeling. If he took this on board he would know that she wanted more of a social life with him. Obviously, knowing how she feels might mean that he has to adjust his life, but this could be preferable to the breakdown of the relationship.

Fiona's strategy should not be to make an accusation, as that will just provoke the type of response that leads to a row. Instead, she needs to explain to Gareth exactly how she feels and why she feels that way. This is more likely to lead to a fruitful discussion and will help to resolve the issue.

If Gareth is not willing to change then Fiona perhaps needs to develop a social life separate from Gareth. She could decide to take an evening class, go out with friends or take up some other activity that will give her the social contact that she needs.

Sensitivity is not only important in very close relationships like

Gareth and Fiona's, it's also valuable in building a rapport with others. At work, for instance, knowing the names of colleagues' partners and children and regular enquiries as to their welfare shows that you see each one as an individual. Similarly, finding out about their interests and hobbies will help you to build relationships and thus improve life at work for you and them.

Being sensitive also means keeping in mind things that are important to other people. Remembering someone's birthday or an anniversary makes all the difference to a relationship, as does doing unexpectedly thoughtful things like giving flowers or arranging a surprise outing.

We all like compliments: they make us feel good and strengthen relationships. Unfortunately, whether it's at home or at work, it's very easy to forget and just use them as occasional social niceties. So, if you don't do it already, get into the habit of recognizing the efforts of those around you by regular comments and compliments.

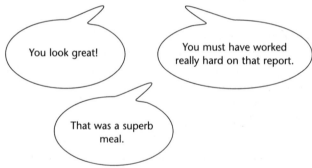

If you are in a close relationship, regularly show your affection. Close contacts such as kisses, cuddles, hugs and holding hands are just as important as lovemaking. A kiss goodbye, the unexpected peck on the cheek or lips and telling your partner you love him or her keeps your relationship alive.

Finally, accept and appreciate others for what they are, not what you'd like them to be. Change comes from within. What you do will undoubtedly influence the way that others act, but you cannot change other people unless they genuinely want that change for themselves. Many relationships come to grief because this is forgotten.

So now take stock. Think about how sensitive you are to those close to you and to other people around you, and jot down your conclusions; Table 5.5 will help you to do this.

**Table 5.5 Becoming more sensitive to others**

| Am I sensitive to others? | Action I need to take |
| --- | --- |
| Do I give others the opportunity to talk about themselves and encourage them to do so? If so, how? | |
| Do I show an interest in other people and their lives? If so, how? | |
| Do I remember important dates like birthdays and anniversaries? | |
| Do I show affection regularly? | |
| Do I remember to compliment, thank and praise others? | |
| Do I generally accept people for what they are, or am I always trying to change them to fit in with what I want? | |

## Don't sulk

Sulking is a 'lose–lose' situation. It's a way of making sure that when you're miserable, everyone else is unhappy. While you punish yourself by carrying around a burden of resentment, those around you have to put up with your brooding and bad temper. There's an example in Box 5.3.

---

### Box 5.3 Sulking

Joe has a problem. His wife Sarah often goes out in the evenings. One night she goes down the local club to play bingo and chat to friends. On another evening she pops over to see her mum. She also does an evening class in Spanish. Although Joe doesn't want to go out he likes to have Sarah around. Here are his thoughts:

> She's arranged to go out again so that I'm on my own all evening. Well, two can play at that game. If she doesn't want to spend her evenings with me, then I'll ignore her.

To express his feelings, Joe resorts to sulking when Sarah is around. He only speaks when spoken to and then only answers briefly and curtly. In bed he avoids physical contact, moving well on to his side of the bed and turning away from Sarah.

---

Sulking often occurs in close relationships but it can also happen in other social situations. For instance, a person might respond to being passed over for a promotion by being surly with colleagues and doing the minimum amount of work he or she can get away with. The aim may be to punish those around, but it also has a personal cost. It leads to loss of job satisfaction and constant negative feelings such as anger and bitterness.

Sulking does not provide solutions for anyone, but unfortunately some people get stuck in this way of operating. If this is you, there are ways out.

To help you to understand this, let's look back at Joe. He has two alternatives. First, he can be open with Sarah. He can let her know how he feels and discuss some possible compromises. Being open about your feelings releases tensions and paves the way for solutions. Sulking does just the opposite: it closes down communication so nothing can be worked out.

But, of course, if Joe's idea of being open about his feelings is just to accuse Sarah, he's not going to get very far.

> *You* never consider me.
> *You're* only interested in
> your own pleasure.

Just using the word 'you' turns what Joe says into an accusation and lays the foundation for conflict. There's a better way of going about things.

> *I* really enjoy your company
> and so *I* get a bit down
> when you're out so often.

Here, Joe is using what we call 'I statements'. By using 'I' and explaining his feelings, he's not accusing Sarah, but asking her to understand his point of view. Sometimes it is necessary to communicate that someone else is behaving in a way that is unacceptable to you. But how you do this will determine their reaction and what follows.

Joe's second option is to change the way he's actually thinking about the situation. In Chapter 2, we saw that feelings come from the way we think. If Joe thought like this, his feelings of resentment would diminish.

> OK, so Sarah is out three evenings a week, but the
> other four she's with me. It's right that she should
> go and see her mum. I can't complain about that. I
> know she enjoys her bingo, but it's not my scene. But
> I wouldn't mind learning a bit of Spanish. It would
> help us on our holidays and we'd have fun practising
> together.

Being open, using 'I statements' and changing the way you think can make a tremendous difference to your relationships. They are positive alternatives to the no-win situation posed by sulking. If you are inclined to sulk about problems and difficulties, it's important to make changes.

So try practising these alternatives.

## Be open to criticism

Positive criticism, although rarely wanted, is necessary. We all make errors and there's nothing wrong with that. It's the way we learn. But it's not very useful to keep making the same mistakes over and over again, and that's where positive criticism is both useful and necessary.

We all know that it's much nicer to be complimented and praised than to have negative judgements passed on us, and it can be particularly galling if in your own mind you'd been doing things right anyway. But part of being a confident person is the ability to rationally examine criticism.

This involves not allowing yourself to get upset, giving it careful consideration and, if necessary, making changes. This is not easy, and if you find this sort of thing particularly difficult to cope with, some practice will help you to deal with future situations.

So first put yourself in a calm state; Box 5.4 tells you how to do this.

---

### Box 5.4 How to calm down

Breathe in slowly to a count of four.

Breathe out slowly to a count of six.

Relax your shoulder muscles.

Relax your stomach muscles.

Repeat this process several times.

---

When you feel calm, try out this exercise. Ask someone you are close to and trust to detail any aspects of your behaviour that he or she finds annoying. Write them down, as in Table 5.6.

**Table 5.6 Am I being annoying?**

| Behaviour described | How do I feel about that comment? Am I open to change? Can I change this behaviour, and if so how? |
|---|---|
|  |  |
|  |  |
|  |  |
|  |  |

Then calmly examine the criticism to decide whether it is valid. If it is, decide how you can correct things.

In future, if you do receive criticism, deal with it in this way. Use the relaxation technique to put yourself into a calm state of mind. Then examine the criticism and, if you feel that it is valid, work out how you can make changes.

## Learn to resolve conflicts

Whatever the nature of the conflict between people, allowing emotions to take over does nothing to resolve the situation. So what we suggest here are some ideas that will help to reduce tensions and allow conflicts to be resolved in a civilized and satisfactory manner.

First, it's important to remember that solutions will not emerge when emotions are running high. Angry people do not think rationally and are usually convinced that they are right. So don't rush into things. Give everyone time to calm down. Accept that a cooling-off period is always a good idea. Then, once things have settled down a bit, agree on a time for sorting things out and use this process.

- Agree that you will all look for a win–win result. That means some gains for everyone, not victory for some and defeat for others. For instance, in the case of Gareth and Fiona (Box 5.2, p. 59), a win–win situation could be that they agree to have certain social evenings out together each week. But also, given Gareth's dedication to football, they might decide to stay in or change the evening if there is a clash with a particularly important match.
- Agree that you will each explain your own position using 'I statements' (these are explained on pp. 63 and 77).
- Agree that you all have a right to state your own opinion and to be listened to.
- Start by each saying something that you like or respect about the others involved in the dispute. This influences all of what follows because, in saying these things, you focus on people rather than the dispute.
- Concentrate on the issues and discuss potential win–win solutions.

One way to get a handle on how others think and feel is to use the 'three chairs' approach. Ask someone who is not involved to act as a facilitator. Each person should be given the chance to try this approach. Others involved in the conflict should not be present. Start by setting up three chairs.

For this to work, each person has to sit in each of the three chairs in turn. In the first chair, you give your own point of view, detailing:

- how you think the situation arose;
- what you think happened;
- what your thoughts and feelings were at the time.

You then move to Chair 2, imagine that you are the other person and try to give the same details from that individual's viewpoint.

In Chair 3, you imagine yourself to be an independent onlooker and try to summarize the conflict from that perspective.

After going through this process, you sit again in Chair 1 as yourself and state whether you see things differently now.

After each person has been through this process with the neutral facilitator, the final step is to seek a resolution of the conflict. Use the method shown on p. 66. Just using the chairs method often leads to better long-term relationships because it develops understanding and empathy, even when there may not be a resolution that satisfies either or both parties.

## Improve your body language

We all communicate both consciously and subconsciously with our bodies. In fact, we register people's body language and pass judgements even before we hear them speak. So it's useful to think about your own body language and make sure that it is consistent with the message that you consciously want to put across. For instance, the lecturer who asks if anyone has any questions while standing with arms folded, legs crossed, jaw jutting forward and an unsmiling face is hardly likely to be taken up. Similarly, if you go for an interview with shoulders hunched and your head looking down, you've already conveyed the message that you are feeling low.

So here are a few things to think about.

- Get your eye contact right. With the right amount of eye contact people generally feel comfortable with each other. Too little eye contact can suggest shiftiness or just timidity or lack of interest. Too much eye contact makes the recipient feel uncomfortable and can be interpreted as aggressive.
- Give sincere smiles. Smiling with your cheeks, mouth, eyes and eyebrows really looks like a smile and conveys genuine happiness or amusement or friendliness. If the eyes and eyebrows are not involved, the smile looks false.
- Keep your head up. This conveys energy and vitality.
- Stand or sit in an open way. This encourages communication. And when you do this, try to use your hands in a symmetrical

way. Gestures such as pointing are a sure way to send out an
aggressive or bossy message.
- Think about your movements. Continually moving your hands
and touching your face a lot can convey nervousness, a lack of
confidence or shiftiness, according to the circumstances.

All this seems a lot to think about, but most of these are things you
probably already do naturally and with confidence. However, if you
want to get your relationships right, it is an area to be aware of and
think about. If you do feel that you have got problems then this is
not something you can sort out on your own. Find someone you
can trust to be honest with you, and ask whether your body language is OK. Ask whether what you say matches the body language
that you use. Using a grid like the one in Table 5.7 may help you to
summarize the answers.

**Table 5.7 Does my body language match my words?**

| Body part | Problem |
| --- | --- |
| Eye contact | |
| Facial expressions | |
| Arms and legs | |
| Hands | |
| Posture | |

## Learn to say 'no'

At times most of us experience overload. If it's just for a limited
time, we usually manage to handle it. But to be weighed down
with too many tasks over a long period leads to constant tension
and a feeling that you're running out of control. This, in turn, can
lead to mental anguish and depression. Overload is, unfortunately,
often a feature of modern life. Driven to succeed and wanting to
please others, many of us take on more than we can really cope

with at work, and skilled managers are often good at exploiting our willingness.

> Lois, you're our best programmer. That's why we'd like you to develop the new site.

> Sanjay, we've decided to upgrade your title to Associate Director. As well as your other work, this will mean staying later to attend after-work meetings with clients.

Our own life expectations also propel us to take on more, and balancing work and home life creates its own headaches.

> I'd like to be at home with Jack, but Sam says we need the money.

> Will you pick up the kids today? I'm just too busy.

If you already have a tendency towards depression, overload is the last thing you need, and so at times you have to learn to say 'no'. How do you do this without creating further problems for yourself? The answer is to act assertively. That is, to say 'no' in a firm but pleasant way using open body language and explaining your reasons. Alternatively, accept only if some of your current responsibilities are transferred to others.

To strengthen your resolve to act assertively, it's a good idea to think back to times when, despite your own misgivings, you gave in to pressure. Use Table 5.8 as a guide to help you with this; copy it out and complete it as many times as you need to.

**Table 5.8 An occasion when I gave in to pressure**

| |
|---|
| *The occasion* |
| |
| What I said and did |
| |
| My feelings |
| |
| How I should have responded |
| |

A simple 'no' to a request is usually insufficient. It is important that you explain your position as well.

For instance, Lois (p. 69) was being asked by her manager to take charge of developing a new website, and he was flattering her by telling her that she was the best programmer. Box 5.5 shows how she could respond, in a firm way and using open body language.

---

**Box 5.5 Lois's response**

'Thanks for calling me your best programmer – that's made me feel good – and I would love the challenge of developing a new site from scratch. The problem is that my time is already fully occupied with other programming that we have already agreed I should do. So, I'm sorry, but taking on the new website is just not possible.'

---

Now, if you can, detail a future situation where you may need to say 'no', using Table 5.9 as a guide. Think about the body language that you will use. Make sure it's open and assertive.

**Table 5.9 Saying 'no'**

*The occasion*

How I will respond in future

To reinforce your decision, use the Stay in Control audio track that you can download from <www.behaviourchange.org> (see the Appendix, p. 105). You will need to read your responses in the previous exercise before using this track so that you can put them into operation in your imagination. If you really have a problem with acting assertively then use the Confronting Fears track, which can be downloaded from the same site.

# 6
# The power of language

In this chapter you will learn to:

- use language to prime yourself to feel generally more positive and to prepare yourself for dealing with specific situations;
- avoid using language that limits your abilities;
- avoid conflict by using 'I statements'.

## Prime yourself for the day

How you begin your day really matters. So, what makes a good start? Well, rushing around and getting uptight when things delay you is clearly not the thing to do. It makes you irritable and even accident-prone. You must allow yourself enough time to get ready, have some breakfast and if necessary deal with any hold-ups calmly. You can also prime yourself to be positive by your use of language.

You may recall the New York University experiments we described in Chapter 1 (see p. 4). There we explained that by manipulating the words used in simple tasks such as unscrambling sentences, experimenters were able to affect their subjects' behaviour. For example, one group primed with words associated with ageing seemed slower in follow-up tests, while another group presented with sentences that included words relating to youth and vitality were more energetic. Further experiments have confirmed these findings, so the lesson is clear: you can prime yourself to have a good day.

Make a start by reading the poem in Box 6.1, by the sixth-century Indian dramatist Kalidasa. It's a helpful primer because it not only focuses the mind on the day ahead, it also emphasizes its significance. It's important to read this poem with feeling. If you like it, why not make a copy and place it somewhere you'll see it each morning?

**Box 6.1  Salutation to the Dawn**

Look to this day,
For it is life,
The very life of life.
In its brief course
Lie all the realities and truths of existence.
The joy of growth,
The splendour of action,
The glory of power.
For yesterday is but a memory,
And tomorrow is only a vision,
But today well lived
Makes every yesterday a memory of happiness,
And every tomorrow a vision of hope.
Look well, therefore, to this day.
Such is the salutation to the dawn

                                                    Kalidasa

It's also important to choose some priming words that are relevant to you and your needs each day. Here's an example of how to do it.

Jack is a trade union official. He thinks about the day ahead and decides how he wants to feel and act. He uses a thesaurus to generate some possible priming words. Table 6.1 summarizes his plans.

**Table 6.1  Jack's priming words**

|  | He wants to | Priming words |
|---|---|---|
| *Situation 1*<br>A shop steward has been sacked and Jack knows that he will be talking to angry people. | Calm the situation down. Show an understanding of what has happened to both sides. Seek a compromise that will allow the shop steward to be reinstated without the management losing face. | Calm<br>Persuasive<br>Fair<br>Even-handed<br>Attentive<br>Conciliatory<br>Sympathetic<br>Solution-oriented |
| *Situation 2*<br>Jack will be involved in pay-bargaining. | Present his case in such a way that the company will find it very hard to deny a reasonable wage rise. | Confident<br>Assertive<br>Firm<br>In control<br>Determined<br>Knowledgeable |

Jack then writes each set of priming words down on a card, which he keeps with him for the day. Before each situation, he rehearses his priming words several times. In this process he will automatically imagine himself behaving in those ways.

Use a grid like the one in Table 6.2 to try this approach yourself. As you say the priming words, imagine each situation going positively in the way that you want. If you do this you'll find that your mind and your body are prepared for the challenges ahead.

**Table 6.2 Preparing for my challenges**

|           | I want to be | Priming words |
| --------- | ------------ | ------------- |
| Situation |              |               |
| Situation |              |               |
| Situation |              |               |
| Situation |              |               |
| Situation |              |               |

This whole process becomes more effective if it is combined with using the Stay in Control audio hypnotherapy track that you can download from <www.behaviourchange.org> (see the Appendix, p. 105).

## Affirmations

These are confident, positive statements used to create self-belief and a certainty that things will turn out well in the future. The early twentieth-century French psychotherapist Emile Coué set a fashion for this. He used to tell his patients to recite the phrase:

Every day, in every way, I'm getting better and better.

It's a simple statement, but very powerful, and is still used by many people to combat feelings of negativity. Of course, there is a danger that phrases like these just become overworked and lose their potency. So it's important for you to learn how to develop your own affirmations – the ones that are effective and compelling for you and address the situation in which you find yourself.

When you construct your affirmations, don't say what you won't do. State them in positive terms. Coué didn't tell people to say, 'I won't get ill any more.' He taught them to say, 'I'm getting better.'

Affirmations work best if, at the same time, you use a visualization. So don't just say, 'I'm going to do really well in my driving test': actually create a picture of your success in your mind. Visualize yourself driving confidently and safely through all manoeuvres involved in the test. Imagine your feelings when you find you've passed.

Here are some examples of the way to express affirmations. Read through them and then think up and record some affirmations that fit you and your life.

| | |
|---|---|
| I can succeed. | I will do well. |
| I am strong enough to . . . | I can handle this. |
| I can . . . | I am determined to . . . |
| This is a great opportunity to . . . | |

## Sending out messages

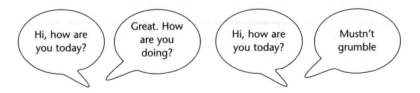

Have you ever noticed how differently people respond to being greeted?

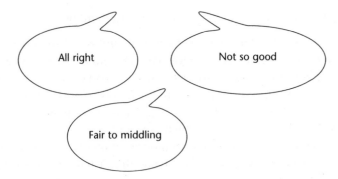

Just the way that you respond to being greeted has an effect on your own frame of mind.

A cheerful 'great', 'fine' or 'good' makes your whole body change. You smile and stand more upright, and subsequent exchanges tend to strike a positive note. But a downbeat 'not so good' or 'reasonable, I suppose' has the opposite effect and either tends to be off-putting or descends into a pessimistic chat about problems.

So what's the lesson here? It is clearly important to be genuine and honest, but don't get into the habit of always giving a downbeat response. Really examine how you feel.

Over the next few days, do a bit of your own research. Notice how others respond to greetings and spot the effect this has. Try and make your own greetings upbeat and watch the results of this.

## Limiting phrases

We all at times say negative things to ourselves.

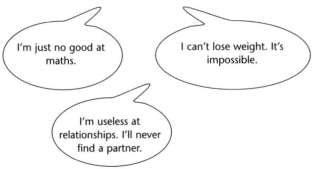

The more these phrases are repeated, the more we come to believe them and the more they limit our development. Often, these 'limiting phrases' begin in childhood in response to a bad experience, but constant repetition turns them into beliefs that are never challenged and so they become self-fulfilling prophecies. Henry Ford recognized this when he said, 'Those who think they can, and those who think they can't, are both right.'

So if you regularly give yourself negative messages, it's time to examine what you are telling yourself. Jotting it down, as in Table 6.3, will help you.

**Table 6.3 My limiting phrases**

| |
| --- |
| My limiting word or phrase |
| Evidence for |
| Evidence against |
| Action needed to change this |

## Use 'I', not 'you'

When another person does or says something that you don't like, it's quite natural to feel resentment. But remember, the words you use in response can intensify your own mood and deepen any conflict. Look at the conversation between Ella and Paul.

Paul, I won't be around for a couple of days. Helen, Clare and I are off on a girls' weekend.

*You* are always doing this sort of thing. *You* never consult me. *You* don't care about our relationship.

Did you notice how often Paul used the word 'you'? Rather than explaining how he feels, this one word leads him to adopt a harsh accusatory tone and means that the exchange is likely to descend into an argument, with each side blaming the other.

Suppose Paul had said, 'I'm not happy about this. I wish we could discuss things before each of us makes arrangements. I'm now going to be at a loose end this weekend.'

Simply using 'I' instead of 'you' changes both the atmosphere and the tenor of the conversation. This approach is less likely to lead to conflict.

Think about this. Could you, by substituting 'I' for 'you', change the way you deal with things you don't like?

# 7

# Happiness

In this chapter, you will learn how to identify some of the factors that influence happiness. You will also consider how happiness can be affected by:

- music;
- the influence of the natural world;
- being absorbed;
- adding something new to your life;
- the balance between mental, physical and social–spiritual aspects of life;
- carrying out kind actions.

## Introduction and self-analysis

Happiness refers to a variety of emotions from contentment through to euphoria. We might also define it as 'an absence of unhappiness'. What is certainly true is that individuals are different and the range of happiness that we experience reflects this.

Early research suggested that, despite changes in circumstances, the happiness of individuals does not generally change over time. This led to the view that happiness levels could not be changed. Fortunately, more recent studies by the American psychologist Martin Seligman have shown this assumption to be false.[12] He suggests that each of us has a band of happiness and that it is possible to 'live in the upper reaches of this set range'.

The happy person is one who not only enjoys the 'now', even if it is a struggle, but also has a sense of meaning and purpose in life.[13] But it is possible to have a sense of purpose and meaning yet not be happy – consider the example in Box 7.1.

---

**Box 7.1 Rajif**

Rajif was a natural sportsman from a young age. He won all the races at school. As a young teenager he joined the local athletics club, his talent was recognized and he trained as a middle-distance runner. His father went along to the club and became his most enthusiastic supporter. Rajif became very successful. But he was training every day and had to study as well. So life was becoming one round of training, competing and studying. He was not enjoying himself but thought that when he started to win the big medals and became famous it would all be worthwhile. Also, his family were so proud of him and he didn't want to let them down. So he had a great sense of purpose without being happy.

---

Some people live their lives this way. They are sure that happiness is around the corner but they never actually attain it. If you recognize an aspect of yourself in this description, perhaps it is time to reflect.

The first step is to think about the things that underpin your happiness and give you satisfaction. They'll probably include your family, friends, a sense of purpose, the way others perceive you and so on. Record the things that underpin your happiness, as in Box 7.2.

---

**Box 7.2 The things that underpin my happiness are ...**

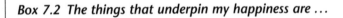

Now, consider the things that give you immediate pleasure. As well as more intense experiences such as the joy of a close relationship, these might include simpler things like the comforts of home, the taste of particular foods, listening to a favourite piece of music, a social evening with friends. Think about these things and then get a sheet of paper and complete some 'Happiness is ...' sentences as below. Remember to think of all your senses – vision, hearing, touch, temperature, taste and smell. Continue on another sheet if necessary.

Happiness is

Happiness is

Happiness is

Happiness is

Happiness is

Happiness is

Happiness is

Happiness is

Happiness is

Happiness is

Happiness is

Happiness is

Happiness is

You've listed some of the things that give you pleasure and your next step is to make sure that the things that make you happy are part of your day-to-day life. Table 7.1 is an example to get you thinking.

**Table 7.1 Example of a happiness plan**

| This makes me happy | Ideas |
|---|---|
| Music | • Buy an iPod and listen to my favourite music while doing jobs at home.<br>• Join the jazz club. |
| Good food | • Once a week prepare a special meal which includes some of my favourite foods.<br>• Enrol on an Italian cookery course. |
| Socializing | • Invite friends round for a meal.<br>• Make sure I have at least one evening out with friends every week. |

Now try this approach for yourself; use Table 7.2 as a guide.

**Table 7.2 My happiness plan**

| This makes me happy | Ideas |
|---|---|
|  |  |
|  |  |
|  |  |
|  |  |

## Use music

It's a well-recognized fact that music can make you feel good. We suggest that you actually identify your own 'feel-good music collection', and by keeping this easily accessible you have a very quick way of uplifting your mood. So what's in your happiness compilation? Write down some of your ideas, as in Box 7.3.

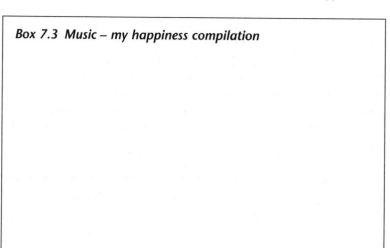

*Box 7.3 Music – my happiness compilation*

Modern technology makes it very easy to keep your music close at hand and instantly playable, so if you are not already into gadgetry, perhaps it's time to find out what's available.

And don't be shy! Just as visualization increases the effects of affirmations, getting into music with your whole body increases its power. So when you can, don't forget to sing along and even dance! If this makes you embarrassed, do it when no one else is around.

Dancing and singing with the music enhance its effect.

## Use your relationship with nature

Look around, and you will see that wherever people live they surround themselves with images of the natural world.

The most obvious of these are the gardens that people create for themselves or the parks and famous gardens that they visit. Indoor plants, vases of flowers, window boxes and curtains, wallpapers and china with images of nature all illustrate this very basic need.

Interestingly, recent research has highlighted this need. In one study, surgery patients who had plants placed in their rooms spent less time recovering, took fewer painkillers and suffered from less pain, anxiety and fatigue than a control group without plants in their rooms.[14]

The mental health charity MIND commissioned a study on the effect on mood and self-esteem of a walk in the country compared to a walk through a shopping centre. The research, carried out by Essex University, showed that, for the great majority, the walk in the country was more effective in raising both measures.[15] They also reported that 94 per cent of the respondents to a survey identified green activities as helping to lift their depression, while 90 per cent linked exercise and contact with nature as their most effective mood raiser.

Perhaps you might like to reflect on this research. Are there any ways in which you can improve your use of this natural mood raiser? Detail your ideas on paper, as in Box 7.4.

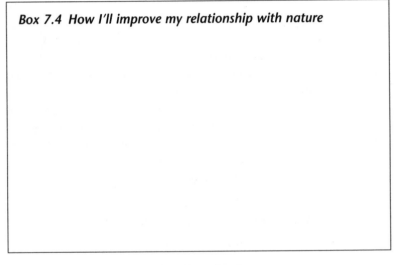

*Box 7.4 How I'll improve my relationship with nature*

## Be absorbed

Have you noticed that when you're really absorbed in something, you don't have time to dwell on your own inner life and feelings? So whenever you are feeling low, this is something to cultivate.

Make a start by thinking about some of the activities that have absorbed you in the past. Revisit those feelings of contentment that you experienced when you were really engrossed in something and unaware of the passing of time. Jot down your memories, using Table 7.3 as a guide.

**Table 7.3 My memories of being engrossed**

| What was it? | My feelings |
| --- | --- |
| | |
| | |
| | |
| | |
| | |

Is it again time to make some of these activities more a part of your life?

## Add something new

Most of us dream about adding new things to our lives, but realizing our ambitions is a different matter. And the excuse is invariably the same.

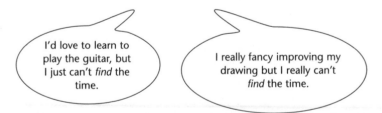

> I'd love to learn to play the guitar, but I just can't *find* the time.

> I really fancy improving my drawing but I really can't *find* the time.

In fact, you don't 'find' time, you 'make' it. It may be that you have to rearrange other aspects of your life, but if adding this new thing will enhance the quality of your life then you should seriously consider it.

It's also important to realize that taking on something new can be an important mood raiser. Although often frustrating at the start, mastering new things can be a lot of fun and also may bring you into contact with new people who have similar interests.

What's more, as you get absorbed in fresh things, your mind relaxes and negative thoughts diminish.

So, is there one new thing that you could add to your life? Something you have always wanted to do but somehow have never got round to? Is it possible to fit this into your life? If you did, would it be necessary to cut out some other activity, and if so what? Copy the grid in Table 7.4 and use it to help you think through your ideas.

**Table 7.4 Something new in my life**

What new activity do I want to introduce into my life?

What physical resources do I need to do this?

Who can help or advise me?

Do I need training and, if so, where and how can I get it?

How much will it cost and can I afford it?

Will I need to remove some other activity in order to make time available and, if so, what should go?

Is taking up this activity going to affect my relationship with someone close to me?

## Live a balanced life

Although each of us is an individual, as human beings we all have the same sorts of needs. We need to:

- keep physically fit and healthy;
- remain mentally alert and able to face life's challenges;
- have a social–spiritual context to our lives through which we can experience an inner peace and sense of belonging. (Here we use 'spiritual' to mean a number of things. This includes a deep personal relationship, contact with nature, a particular belief system or simply a meditative experience.)

Happiness is about getting the balance right between the physical, the mental and the social–spiritual sides of life. Depression, on the other hand, is often a warning sign that these are actually out of balance. Box 7.5 is an example of someone who got it wrong.

---

**Box 7.5 Darren**

Darren is ambitious and determined to make a good impression in his new job. He works very long hours, but still wants to be a caring husband and father. So he never lets up. Because he's in a hurry he often skips breakfast and lunch and is on the go all day. He doesn't have time for exercise, having a beer with friends or even time on his own.

---

Have you got the balance right? Use a grid like the one in Table 7.5 to list the things that contribute to the physical, mental and social–spiritual facets of your life. Then give yourself a score out of ten for each aspect.

**Table 7.5 Is my life balanced?**

| Physical | |
|---|---|
| | Score |

| Mental | |
|---|---|
| | Score |

| Social–spiritual | |
|---|---|
| | Score |

If you are not happy with the results, decide on some changes.

## Care for others

Another interesting point about happiness is that it's not just about self-gratification. Psychologist Martin Seligman suggested an interesting course of action to one of his student groups. He proposed that over the next couple of weeks, each student should carry out one philanthropic activity and one pleasurable one. He also asked them to record their mood during and after each event. The results were, in his words, 'life-changing'. Many participants reported that 'the afterglow of the pleasurable activity paled in comparison with the effects of a kind action'.[16] Some students described feeling better for the whole day, and one admitted to being amazed to find that he enjoyed helping people more than spending money!

Without sermonizing, the lesson from this is obvious: the giver as well as the receiver has a lot to gain from generosity. Depression is by its very nature inward-looking. It focuses on inner feelings rather than the world around. So this might be a way to change this imbalance.

Try this out for yourself. Think up two activities, one that is just pleasurable to you and one that involves helping others, and record what you are going to do, using Table 7.6 as a guide. Monitor your mood while doing them, and then score your feelings as each is completed and for the rest of the day.

**Table 7.6  My responses to two activities**

Activity involving helping someone else

|  |  |
| --- | --- |
|  | Score |

Pleasurable activity

|  |  |
| --- | --- |
|  | Score |

# 8

## Sleep solutions

This chapter will consider some general points about sleep and its relationship to anxiety and rumination. It also provides some useful tips for better sleep and gives you the opportunity to develop your own sleep plan.

Waking up in the morning but still feeling tired is a common symptom of depression. There are changes in the patterns of sleep in depression, with a greater amount of time being spent in Rapid Eye Movement (REM) sleep, where the brain activity is similar to a waking state. It is as though the brain does not shut down enough to allow deep, restful sleep. The root cause of these changed sleep patterns appears to be the anxiety that is created by a constant daily routine of going over and over worrying things. It is as though the brain continues with this rumination, and the consequent anxiety, during sleep.

Clearly, one of the best solutions is to stop ruminating, and strategies for doing this are provided in other chapters in this book. However, this will require some practice, and until you have conquered that habit we suggest that every evening you use the Sleep audio hypnotherapy track that you can download from <www.behaviourchange.org> (see Appendix, p. 105, for further details). This will help you to put away all those anxieties, relax you and prepare you for a restful, deep sleep.

There are many other changes that you may need to make to improve the quality of your sleep. They relate to your lifestyle, your general state of physical fitness, use of stimulants, and so on. Some of these may be very important factors. For instance, a reduction in the general level of anxiety can, in some people, be brought about by reducing or cutting out caffeine intake. In Box 8.1 and the following pages we have included some sleep tips.

*Box 8.1 Sleep tips*

*Exercise*

Regular physical activity like gardening, walking and sports are important for healthy sleep.

So make sure that you consistently include some form of exercise in your daily routines.

*Eat well*

You should be eating a good balanced diet with plenty of fruit and vegetables.

Eat your largest meals well before bedtime. Ideally, the main one should be at midday, but if that's not possible have it at least three hours before retiring.

Since carbohydrates are important for good sleep, eat high protein meals earlier in the day and more carbohydrates later.

Fatty or spicy food should not be eaten in the evening.

*Reduce your caffeine intake*

You shouldn't drink more than three or four cups of tea or coffee a day, and coffee should really be just a morning drink. Only caffeine-free drinks should be consumed in the evening.

## Aids to a good night's sleep

- *Organize your evening* to make sure that you get to bed at the best time for you. It's also a good idea to be fully organized for the next day so that you can go to bed with a relaxed mind.
- *Wind down before bedtime.* Stop work or any stimulating activity a couple of hours before bedtime and do something relaxing like listening to music, watching television or reading a book. Whatever you choose, make sure it isn't too stimulating (movies with lots of action are not a good idea – you can watch those another time!)

- *Take a warm bath or shower.* This relaxes your muscles and pre-pares you for sleep.
- *Use the Sleep session.* Download from <www.behaviourchange.org> (see Appendix, p.105 for full details). It's designed to help you put away all of the anxieties of the day and gently relax into sleep so that you wake up feeling refreshed and rejuvenated. Try and use it in bed, not when you are sitting in a chair. Ideally you will fall asleep before the sleep track finishes or shortly after, so it would be useful to have an audio player that can be programmed to play just the one track.

## What to avoid

- *Don't lie there tossing and turning.* If you really can't get to sleep, get up. Wrap yourself up to stay warm, have a hot caffeine-free drink and read something light and relaxing until you begin to feel tired again. Then go back to bed not worrying about whether you will go to sleep immediately.
- *Don't use sleeping pills.* They just complicate matters.
- *Don't use alcohol to get you to sleep.* It damages the quality of your sleep, and in many cases it causes early waking accompanied by sweating, increased heart rate and restlessness. For good, long-term sleep health, drink no more that one glass of beer or wine per day and ensure that it is consumed at least three hours before bedtime.

## Seasonal affective disorder

Seasonal affective disorder (SAD) is the lowering of mood that occurs in some people when the days get shorter in the autumn. It lasts until the days increase in length again. This is normally around the beginning of March, but for some people the low mood remains beyond this. It's unknown below the 30th parallel (30 degrees north of the equator) because the seasonal change in the length of the day is so small.

The ancient Greeks were aware of this seasonal lowering of mood, but it is only in the last 50 years that it has been investigated. The term 'seasonal affective disorder' was introduced in 1984, and the

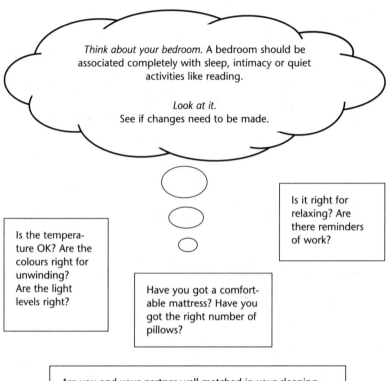

*Think about your bedroom.* A bedroom should be associated completely with sleep, intimacy or quiet activities like reading.

*Look at it.*
See if changes need to be made.

Is it right for relaxing? Are there reminders of work?

Is the temperature OK? Are the colours right for unwinding? Are the light levels right?

Have you got a comfortable mattress? Have you got the right number of pillows?

Are you and your partner well matched in your sleeping habits? If not, can you come to a mutually acceptable compromise?

publicity it has received since then has enabled many people to recognize that their own symptoms could fit into this category.

As the days shorten, individuals who have SAD lose interest in socializing and sex. They feel more and more empty and can sleep for up to four hours longer than normal. However, unlike many people suffering from depression, their appetite is not depressed, and in fact they often overeat and gain weight.

The daily sleep–wake cycle is controlled by a brain hormone called melatonin. In people who experience SAD, melatonin is secreted for a longer period than in other people. But the good news is that there's a solution – light. Not any light but a very bright one, first thing in the morning.

Light boxes that produce up to 10,000 lux of white light are commercially available. From early autumn through to the start of spring, someone with SAD needs to sit close to this light for up to 45 minutes each day. For most people, first thing in the morning is usually the right time, so it could be combined with having breakfast or reading the paper. However, the 'best time' actually relates to the pattern of melatonin secretion in each individual, so if you do decide to use a light box you may need to experiment.

## Create a sleep plan

Jot down a few ideas for improving the quality of your sleep and then put these into a sleep plan. Here's a suggested format.

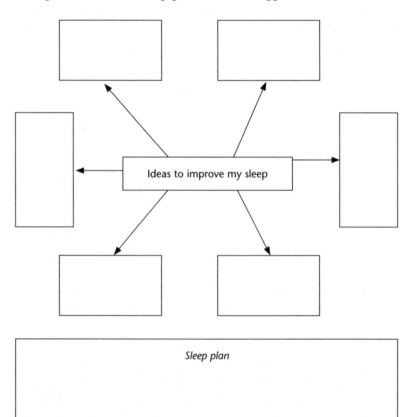

Ideas to improve my sleep

*Sleep plan*

# 9

# The big picture revisited

This chapter will give you the chance to reanalyse your position after having worked through this book. It also helps you to consider any further action.

In Chapter 2, you were asked to look at your own life and identify both the good things and the problems. As you worked through the following chapters, you have hopefully begun to make some changes. But now it's time to take stock again. Look back at your initial assessment. Then copy out the grid in Table 9.1 and fill it in.

**Table 9.1 My progress**

| |
| --- |
| *Areas where I've begun to make changes* |
| |
| *These things have improved* |
| |
| *These are still problems* |
| |
| *Areas that I still need to work on* |
| |

It's possible that some problems may not have been solved because they require you to make major changes in your life, like changing jobs or ending a relationship. Clearly, important changes like these cannot be taken lightly and you may benefit from visiting an experienced counsellor to discuss the issues. You also need to remember that a period of stress may precipitate another bout of depression. So don't rush into anything.

The next few pages will help you to think through some of these more difficult decisions. We have chosen two such decisions – changing jobs and a relationship change – to use as examples of approaches that can be used. The same approaches can be used for other difficult decisions.

Before working through either of the examples, remind yourself of the things that make you happy and write them down, as in Box 9.1. Then go on to the examples: copy out Tables 9.2 and 9.3 and make a record of your responses.

*Box 9.1 Things that make me happy*

**Table 9.2 Changing my job**

*Should I change jobs?*

Why am I doing this job now?

_____

_____

_____

_____

What other jobs are open to me?

_____

_____

_____

_____

Is there a job that I want to do but would need training for?
(If there is, detail the training with, if possible, cost and time.)

_____

_____

_____

_____

_____

Would a change of job have financial implications?

_____

_____

_____

_____

_____

**Table 9.2 continued**

*The consequences of changing my job*

If I changed my job, would there be other consequences? If so, what would they be?

_____

_____

_____

_____

Can I negotiate a different job where I currently work, and if so what would be the consequences for me?

_____

_____

_____

_____

If I did take another job, would this present any problems?

_____

_____

_____

_____

Who should I discuss this idea with?

_____

_____

_____

_____

Other thoughts

_____

_____

_____

## Table 9.3 Making a relationship change

*Should I make a relationship change?*

We are assuming here that this is a close relationship like marriage or long-term partnership. This can be a very major step, involving trauma for everyone involved.

Look back to the chapter on relationships to make sure that you have seriously tried to make your relationship work. Have you and your partner both explored ways of rebuilding your relationship? Surveys of divorced people have shown that many regret the decisions they took to end their marriage. Have you seen a Relate counsellor?

What steps have I taken to make the relationship work?

_____

_____

_____

_____

_____

_____

What would be the effect on my partner of a break-up?

_____

_____

_____

_____

_____

What would be the effect on my family?

_____

_____

_____

_____

_____

**Table 9.3 continued**

*Effects of a relationship change*

What would be the financial effect of a break-up?

_____

_____

_____

_____

_____

_____

_____

Can I cope with such a change in my life and, if so, how?

_____

_____

_____

_____

_____

_____

_____

Further thoughts

_____

_____

_____

_____

_____

_____

_____

_____

It sometimes helps to actually draw up a list of the advantages and disadvantages of a particular course of action. You might like to use the headings in Table 9.4.

**Table 9.4 Advantages and disadvantages**

What I am considering

Advantages

- 
- 
- 
- 
- 
- 

Disadvantages

- 
- 
- 
- 
- 
-

Memories and imagination can also help you to come to the right decision. Table 9.5 shows you how.

**Table 9.5  Using memories and imagination**

| | |
|---|---|
| Step 1 | Close your eyes and allow your mind to go back to a time when you made a decision that was right for you. Think about how you felt at the time – the sensations in your body; your emotions; the thoughts going through your head. |
| Step 2 | Now think about the change you are considering making. Imagine that you have already carried out that change. Think about all the consequences you have outlined. How does it feel? How does it compare with the feelings you experienced a few moments ago during Step 1? |
| Step 3 | Imagine now that you have decided not to make the change. Think about all the consequences you have outlined. How does it feel? How does it compare with the feelings you experienced during Step 1? |

Write down below how you felt at each step

1



2



3

## Some final thoughts

This book needs you to do some work! Change will not come about just by reading through the pages. It will come from working consistently on the exercises outlined. Some behaviours will change easily, but the more established will take time and effort to change.

Remember:

1  Don't try to change everything at once. Choose one or two things and work on them consistently.
2  Make time each day for any psychological or physical exercises you have decided upon.
3  Be ready to constantly challenge your own Automatic Negative Thoughts (ANTs). These could even relate to whether it is worth making changes.
4  If possible, persuade someone close to you to support you. In particular, get him or her to spot and challenge your ANTs.
5  Remember that:

   The way you think influences the way you feel and you *can* change the way you think.

6  Be sensitive to your body and use it to help with mood changes.
7  Your use of language can help to uplift your own mood and provide ways to improve your relationships with others.
8  Establish quality relationships with those around you.
9  Don't just use one approach; combine them.
10  Save the hypnotherapy tracks that you have downloaded from <www.behaviourchange.org> on to an audio player and use them to back up behaviour changes.
11  Be prepared to revisit sections of this book and rework them until the changes you make become part of you.

We wish you well and trust that this book will enable you to achieve a better life.

# Appendix

## Hypnotherapy tracks

Somewhere between sleep and wakefulness lies a deep state of relaxation that can be accessed by hypnosis. During this condition of altered consciousness, the mind is more open to suggestion. While working through this book, you will have identified the changes you want to make. You may also have recognized some good ways of making these changes, but using hypnosis could give you a further means to strengthen your resolve and actually help you to make adjustments to your life.

We have prepared three audio tracks for you to use. They are:

- Confronting Fears
- Stay in Control
- Sleep.

These can be downloaded free from <www.behaviourchange.org> and you can then copy it to the audio player of your choice.

It is important to understand that under no circumstances should you ever use a hypnotherapy track in a car. It should only ever be used while relaxing in a safe environment.

When you are ready to use a track, find a quiet spot to play it through. Sit, preferably with your head supported, or lie down, whichever is more comfortable. Remove items such as your glasses or watch, if these are likely to distract you, and loosen any tight articles of clothing.

Obviously, the Sleep track is designed to prepare you for sleep, but the other two tracks will work best if you are alert. So try not to use them when you are tired.

## Hypnosis track – Confronting Fears

Before you use this track, reread the section on anxiety. You'll find this in Chapter 4, on pp. 37–9. You should deal first with the fear that causes you the least anxiety. When you've taken care of that issue, you can then move on to your next fear. Leave the worst one till last.

For the best results, try and use the track just before confronting your fear. If that's not possible, you can use it up to 24 hours before you have to meet the problem. For things that make you really anxious, you might need a longer build-up. In this situation, use the track each day for several days in a row, including the day before. Finally, use it again on the day itself.

## Hypnosis track – Stay in Control

You can use this track to manage your emotions, to decrease general levels of anxiety, to prepare for the day ahead or for a particular situation such as an interview. Before you use it, reread the section on the power of language. You'll find this in Chapter 6, on pp. 72–8.

You should then think carefully about the day ahead. Decide how you want to feel and how you want to behave in the morning, afternoon and evening. Next, think of a range of priming words and statements and jot them down. Remember, you are preparing yourself for how you want to feel and how you want to behave. So make your words and statements specific to you and to your particular circumstances.

## Hypnosis track – Sleep

This is to help you to get to sleep, so listen to it in bed. You must also use it on a device that will play just this one track and then switch itself off. Before you do listen to it, you need to have read Chapter 8, on sleep solutions. This can be found on pp. 90–5.

# Notes

1 Seligman, Martin E. P., *Learned Optimism*. Pocket Books, New York, 1991.

2 Beck, A. T., *Cognitive Therapy and the Emotional Disorders*. International Universities Press, New York, 1976.

3 Gladwell, Malcolm, *Blink: The power of thinking without thinking*. Allen Lane, London, 2005, pp. 206–7.

4 Alladin, A. and Alibhai, A., 'Cognitive Hypnotherapy for Depression: An empirical investigation'. *International Journal of Clinical and Experimental Hypnosis* 55 (2) (April 2007): 147–66.

5 Seligman, *Learned Optimism*.

6 Beck, *Cognitive Therapy and the Emotional Disorders*.

7 Gladwell, *Blink*, pp. 206–7.

8 Fentem, P. H., 'Benefits of Exercise in Health and Disease'. *British Medical Journal* 308 (1994): 1291–5.

9 Geary, Amanda, *The Mind Guide to Food and Mood*. MIND, the National Association for Mental Heath, London, 2000, rev. edn 2004 (available online at <www.mind.org.uk> and <www.foodandmood.org>).

10 Williams, A. L. *et al.*, 'Do Essential Fatty Acids Have a Role in the Treatment of Depression?' *Journal of Affective Disorders* 93 (1–3) (July 2006): 117–23.

11 Yehuda, S., Rabinovitz, S. and Mostofsky, D. I., 'Mixture of Essential Fatty Acids Lowers Test Anxiety'. *Nutritional Neuroscience* 8 (4) (August 2005): 265–7.

12 Seligman, Martin E. P., *Authentic Happiness*. Nicholas Brealey Publishing, London, 2003.

13 Ben-Shahar, Tal, *The Question of Happiness*. iUniverse, Lincoln, NE, 2001 (also available as an e-book).

14 Ulrich, R. S., 'Health Benefits of Gardens in Hospitals'. Paper for international conference *Plants for People*, 2002 (available online at <https://www.planterra.com/SymposiumUlrich.pdf>).

15 MIND, *Ecotherapy: The green agenda for mental health*. MIND, London, May 2007.

16 Seligman, *Authentic Happiness*.

# Bibliography

Ball, Nigel and Hough, Nick, *The Sleep Solution. Improve your sleep, health and quality of life – from tonight.* Vermilion, London, 1988.

Bandler, Richard and Grinder, John, *Frogs into Princes: Neuro linguistic programming.* Eden Grove Editions, London, 1979.

Ben-Shahar, Tal, *The Question of Happiness.* iUniverse, Lincoln, NE, 2001 (also available as an e-book).

Coleman, Daniel, *Emotional Intelligence.* Bantam Books, London, 1995.

Gentry, W. Doyle, *Anger-Free: Ten basic steps to managing your anger.* Quill–HarperCollins, New York, 1999.

Gillett, Richard, *Overcoming Depression: A practical self-help guide to prevention and treatment.* Dorling Kindersley, London, 1987.

Gladwell, Malcolm, *Blink: The power of thinking without thinking.* Allen Lane, London, 2005.

Glasser, William, *Reality Therapy.* Harper and Row, London, 1965.

Glasser, William, *Choice Theory.* Harper Perennial, London, 1998.

Goldstein, Arnold, P., Glick, B. and Gibbs, J., *Aggression Replacement Training.* Research Press, Champaign, IL, 1998.

Greenberger, Dennis and Padesky, Christine A., *Mind over Mood: Change how you feel by changing the way you think.* Guilford Press, New York, 1995.

Griffin, Joseph and Tyrrell, Ivan, *Breaking the Cycle of Depression: A revolution in psychology.* H. G. Publishing for the European Therapy Studies Institute, Chalvington, Sussex, 2000.

Lewis, Gwyneth, *Sunbathing in the Rain: A cheerful book about depression.* Flamingo HarperCollins, London, 2002.

Maraki, M., Tsofliou, F., Pitsiladis, Y. P., Malkova, D., Mutrie, N. and Higgins, S., 'Acute Effects of a Single Exercise Class on Appetite, Energy Intake and Mood. Is there a time of day effect?' *Appetite* 45 (3) (2005): 272–8.

Matthews, Andrew, *Making Friends.* Media Masters, Singapore, 1990.

O'Connor, Joseph, *NLP Workbook: The practical guide to achieving the results you want.* Thorsons, New York, 2001.

Park, S.-H., 'Randomized Clinical Trials Evaluating Therapeutic Influences of Ornamental Indoor Plants in Hospital Rooms on Health Outcomes of Patients Recovering from Surgery'. PhD dissertation, Kansas State University, 2006.

Pinel, John P., *Biopsychology.* Allyn and Bacon, New York, 2003, fifth edn.

Quilliam, Susan, *Staying Together: From crisis to deeper commitment.* Transformation Management and Relate, London, 1995.

Reeder, Darcy M., 'Cognitive Therapy of Anger Management: Theoretical and practical considerations'. *Archives of Psychiatric Nursing* 5 (3) (1991): 147–50.

Richo, David, *How to Be an Adult in Relationships: The five keys to mindful loving*. Shambhala, Boston and London, 2002.

Schoch, Richard, *The Secrets of Happiness*. Profile Books, London, 2007.

Seligman, Martin E. P., *Learned Optimism*. Pocket Books, New York, 1991.

Seligman, Martin E. P., *The Optimistic Child*. Harper Perennial, London, 1995.

Seligman, Martin E. P., *Authentic Happiness: Using the new positive psychology to realize your potential for lasting fulfilment*. Nicholas Brealey Publishing, London, 2003.

Van de Weyer, Courtney, *Changing Diets, Changing Minds. How food affects mental well-being and behaviour*. Sustain, the Alliance for Better Food and Farming, London, 2005.

Waxman, David, *Hartland's Medical and Dental Hypnosis*. Baillière Tindall, Oxford, 1989.

Yapko, Michael D., *Breaking the Patterns of Depression*. Broadway Books, New York, 1997.

Yapko, Michael D., *Hand-Me-Down Blues: How to stop depression from spreading in families*. St Martin's Griffin, New York, 1999.

Yapko, Michael D., *Treating Depression with Hypnosis. Integrating cognitive–behavioural and strategic approaches*. Brunner-Routledge, Hove, 2001.

# Index

actions
  assessing 101
  from negative thoughts 11–14
alcohol 5, 33
anger 34–7
anxiety 37–9
appearance 43–4

Beck, Aaron T. 3, 10
bereavement 8
blame 27–8
body language
  improving 67–8
  listening 57–8
*British Medical Journal* 45

caffeine
  mind-body relationship 5
  sleep and 91
change
  self-assessment 95–103
  taking slowly 1
cognitive behaviour therapy (CBT)
  3, 10–11
  maintaining with hypnotherapy
    5–6
  relationships and 54
Coué, Emile 74–5
counselling 54
criticism
  receiving 64–5

depression
  defining 1
  five principles and 2–5

education 8
Ellis, Albert 10
exercise
  nature and 84
  sleep and 91

feelings
  from negative thoughts 11–14
five principles 2–5

food and nutrition
  additives 49
  comfort eating 49–52
  effect on mood 47–9
  essential fatty acids 49
  mind-body interaction 33, 47–52
  sleep and 91

Gladwell, Malcolm
  *Blink* 4

happiness
  absorbing activities 84–5
  balance 87–8
  care for others 88–9
  defining for yourself 79–82
  music and 82–3
  nature 83–4
  new interests 85–6
health 8
hypnotherapy
  anger and 37
  audio tracks 105–6
  language 72
  maintaining CBT 5–6
  self-hypnosis 45–6

imagination 102
  positive use of 3, 5

Kalidasa 72–3

language
  affirmations 74–5
  interacting with 75–8
  moods and 2, 4
  priming the day 72–4
listening 56–8
loneliness 8

medications
  sleeping pills 92
meditation 44–5
MIND 48, 84
mind-body interaction 3, 4–5, 33
  anger and 34–7

mind-body interaction (continued)
   anxiety 37–9
   exercise 46–7
   keeping an even keel 40–1
   meditation 44–5
   motivation 42–3
   posture 41
   self-hypnosis 45–6
   smiling 39–40
   your appearance 43–4
   *see also* food and nutrition; sleep
moods
   highs and lows 40–1
   language and 2, 4
motivation 42–3
music 82–3

nature 83–4

optimism and pessimism
   weighing evidence 22–4

relationships 8
   body language and 57–8, 67–8
   caring for others 88–9
   exercise companions 47
   family 8
   importance of 2, 3–4
   listening 56–8
   making changes 99–100
   receiving criticism 64–5
   resolving conflicts 65–7
   saying 'no' 68–71
   self-assessment 53–6
   sensitivity to others 59–61

sulking 61–4
   support from 1–2
retirement 8

seasonal affective disorder (SAD)
   92–4
self-perception
   assessing yourself 28–30
   identifying problems 7–9
   limiting phrases 76–7
   success and self-criticism 30–2
Seligman, Martin 88
sleep 90–3
   creating a plan 94
   SAD and 93–4
sport 8, 47

therapy 54
   *see also* hypnotherapy
thinking
   Automatic Negative Thoughts
     3, 15–20, 103
   catastrophizing 24–6
   challenging 11–20
   controlling 2, 3
   negative thoughts 10–11
   ruminating 20–2, 90
   weighing evidence 22–4
   *see also* change; cognitive
     behaviour therapy

underachievement 8

work 8
   changing 97–8